NOTABLE BOATS

Forty remarkable craft,
forty great adventures

NOTABLE BOATS

NIC COMPTON

with illustrations by PETER SCOTT

IVY PRESS

First published in the UK in 2016 by

Ivy Press

Ovest House, 58 West Street

Brighton BN1 2RA, UK

www.quartoknows.com

British Library Cataloguing-in-Publication Data

A catalogue record for this book is available from the British Library

This book was conceived, designed and produced by

Ivy Press

Publisher *Susan Kelly*

Creative Director *Michael Whitehead*

Editorial Director *Tom Kitch*

Project Editor *Jamie Pumfrey*

Commissioning Editor *Kate Shanahan*

Designer *Ginny Zeal*

Watercolour Artworks *Peter Scott*

Boat Plans *John Woodcock*

Route Maps *Nick Rowland*

ISBN: 978-1-78240-415-6

Printed in China

10 9 8 7 6 5 4 3 2

Contents

Introduction

SEVERAL TIMES A YEAR, when I was editor of *Classic Boat*, I would be asked the question, "What is a classic boat?" We could have filled the magazine many times over with various experts' views about what constitutes a "classic" and still not arrived at a satisfactory definition. Was it the age of the boat? Its design? The materials it was made of? Or just "a feeling?" It took me a while to realize that this very ambiguity was our greatest strength as it gave us latitude to include whatever we wanted. At the end of the day, "classic" is a subjective term, whatever the experts say.

So I have a strange feeling of *déjà vu* as I set out to introduce this selection of *Notable Boats*. What is a "notable boat?" Why, out of all the boats in the world, have we selected these ones? What makes them so especially notable? A dictionary is always a good place to start if you're looking for a definition, and this is what the *Oxford English Reference Dictionary* has to say on the matter:

> notable / ˌnəʊtəb(ə)l / adj. worthy of note; striking, remarkable, eminent.

Using this definition, we could have filled the book 100 times over with notable boats, and it soon became clear that choosing such a small selection of craft was going to be a subjective process. So, to narrow things down a little, we came up with our own criteria.

What was clear was that each boat must have made an interesting or even an historic voyage (the circumnavigators), or have contributed in some way to the history of sailing (*America, Avenger*), or perhaps played a key part in a notable or eminent person's life

(John Lennon, Casanova). The boats should not be too large—we could easily have filled the book with historic ships such as the *Mayflower* and the *Cutty Sark*, but then we would have had to rename it *Notable Ships*. If anything, they should err toward the smaller end of the spectrum, as it is on these boats that so many tales of human endeavor are enacted. We also wanted a mix of new and old, big and small, real and fictional. Apart from that, we were free to choose any boat that was "worthy of note; striking, remarkable, and eminent." What a treat.

The collection of boats in these pages is undoubtedly eclectic (at least one is not even a boat but a raft), and we hope all the more interesting for it. The smallest is *Said*, an 11ft 10in (3.6m) microcruiser which the inimitable Evgeny Gvozdev built on the balcony of his apartment in Dagestan and then sailed around the world at an average speed of 2 knots (3.7km/h). It took him four years. The biggest is the legendary Grand Banks schooner *Bluenose* which became a symbol of national pride in Canada and still features on one of the country's coins. Her very name is a reference to the colloquial term ("bluenosers") for the people of Nova Scotia, where she was built.

Between these two extremes, there are all manner of craft sailing between the covers of this book. There are dinghies, such as the real-life *Swallow* ("the best little boat that ever was built") from the eponymous *Swallows and Amazons* books, that have inspired several generations of sailors to go messing about in boats. There's the *Chidiock Tichbone*, 18ft (5.5m) Drascombe Lugger, which Webb Chiles capsized in the middle of the Pacific but carried on regardless to sail three-quarters of the way around the world. And few vessels of any size have been as overladen with symbolism as the simple raft on which Huckleberry Finn and Jim drifted down the Mississippi and, far from the prejudices of mainstream society, became best of friends. A raft of freedom, nature, equality, innocence, and hope, all wrapped up in a few pegged-together boards of wood.

There are great voyages aplenty, be it the epic circumnavigations of Francis Chichester, Robin Knox-Johnston, and Bernard Moitessier, the leisurely cruises of America's most eminent cruising couple, Lin and Larry Pardy, or the more obscure polar expeditions of Amyr Klink—one of the few people who can boast of having sailed "from Pole to Pole." Some boats achieve fame by sailing much shorter distances, such as the yacht *America*, which raced 53 miles (98km) around the UK's Isle of Wight in 1851 and whose name has been on yachting's most coveted prize, the America's Cup, ever since. And what about the former rescue boat *Christiania*, which sank 1,500ft (450m) to the bottom of the North Sea and then sat there for 20 months before being craned back up and restored? Not many boats can boast of having sailed to the seabed and back again.

From the personal to the political; from one person's inner journey to a whole nation's cultural identity. These themes are repeated throughout the book, where private ambition often sits side by side with a bigger agenda. When the crew of *Dorade* returned to the United States after winning both the Transatlantic and Fastnet races, they were given a ticker-tape parade through New York and thousands of people lined the streets to see them. Good news was in short supply at the time, and the city was looking for heroes. Francis Chichester's triumphant voyage on *Gipsy Moth IV* (which he famously hated) did much to bolster British pride at a time when the country was coming to terms with losing most of its empire. More recently, the voyage of the *Hōkūle'a* from Hawaii to Tahiti brought an end to 500 years of Western arrogance—from the Portuguese explorers onwards—by proving such craft were capable of far more than had previously been imagined.

And there are the global record breakers too. The first solo circumnavigation of the Earth was successfully completed in 1898 by American seaman Joshua Slocum, in a gaff sloop oyster boat named *Spray*. The journey was so daring and dangerous that it wasn't attempted again for over forty years. The epic voyage as detailed in his book *Sailing Alone Around the*

World has provided inspiration for countless ocean adventurers including Ellen MacArthur, who smashed the single-handed round-the-world record in 2005 on the diminutive 21ft (6.3m) sloop *Iduna*, which she had sailed around Britain ten years earlier, a voyage that laid the foundations for everything that followed. More recently, Dutch teenager Laura Dekker took on the authorities in her determination to be the youngest person to sail around the world, successfully navigating *Guppy* to take the record at the age of 16 years and 123 days old.

On the whole, this book shuns celebrity yachts on the basis that they are generally only famous because of their owners and haven't made any journeys worth talking about. But who could resist the story of Casanova escaping the Doge's Palace on a gondola? And, improbable as it seems, John Lennon's three-day trip to Bermuda on the *Megan Jaye* did seem to bring about a genuine transformation. Soon after, he broke his silence and released *Double Fantasy*, the final album he made before his sudden death.

More to our liking was Stephen Ladd who, when he got bored of his job as a city planner, built a 12ft (3.65m) dinghy and set off down the Missouri River toward the Gulf of Mexico, through the Panama Canal, up over the Andes (by lorry), down the Orinoco River and back home via the Caribbean, eventually traveling 15,000 miles (28,000km). Now that is worthy of note, striking, and remarkable—though possibly not eminent, as no one else seems to have heard of him. And there's the 60-year-old Wilfried Erdmann, who sailed four times around the world — three times single-handed; twice single-handed and non-stop; and once single-handed, non-stop, and the wrong way—and yet is barely known outside his native Germany.

In the end, this is of course a subjective selection and there are inevitably any number of eminent boats that didn't make the cut. Like beauty, "notability" is in the eye of the beholder. But as long as you enjoy reading the stories that follow, then that will be reason enough to have included them. And hopefully no one will need to ask me, "What is a notable boat?"

Spray

She was built to dredge for oysters on the Chesapeake Bay, but ended up sailing 46,000 miles (85,000km) around the world. More than a century later, Spray still provides inspiration for countless ocean travelers dreaming of embarking on their own adventures.

JOURNEY: Boston, Massachusetts, to Newport, Rhode Island, via the world
BOAT NAME: *Spray*
CAPTAIN: Joshua Slocum
DATE: 1895–98
DISTANCE: 46,000 nautical miles (85,000km)

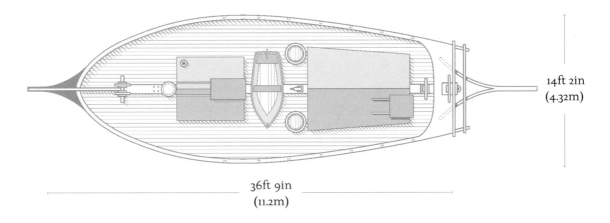

14ft 2in
(4.32m)

36ft 9in
(11.2m)

LENGTH: 36ft 9in (11.2m)
BEAM: 14ft 2in (4.32m)
DRAFT: 4ft 2in (1.27m)
DISPLACEMENT: 18.1 tons (16.4 tonnes)

DATE BUILT: Unknown
RIG: Gaff sloop, yawl after 1885
CREW: 1

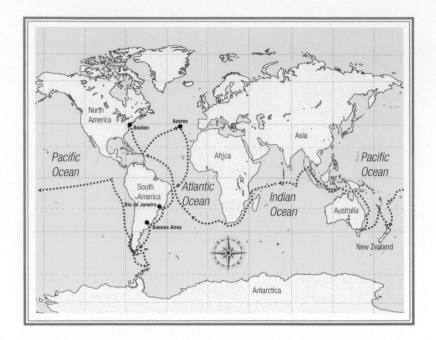

The Granddaddy of Them All
Spray

★ ★ ★

HE'S THE GRANDDADDY OF THEM ALL: the original world-girdling single-handed sailor, revered by all those who followed in his wake. So far ahead of his time was he that his voyage wouldn't be attempted again for another 40 years. Yet it was by pure chance that Joshua Slocum stumbled across the boat that would make him famous. After a lifetime working on sailing ships, first as captain then as master of his own vessels, Slocum washed up in Boston in 1890. He had survived all kinds of dramas at sea, from shipwrecks to mutinies, even the loss of one of his children aboard ship, but it was the advent of steam that finally spelled the end of his career. He simply could not adapt to motor propulsion.

While he was "cogitating" his future, an old acquaintance rolled up and offered him a ship, though he warned, "she wants some repairs." The vessel in question was an old oyster sloop called *Spray*, which Slocum spent the next 13 months rebuilding. She was not the obvious choice for a round-the-world voyage: beamy and flat-bottomed, she was better suited to carrying heavy loads in coastal water than making long passages across open oceans. Despite her apparent limitations, Slocum declared, "she sat on the water like a swan," and on April 24, 1895, set off on his historic voyage. "A thrilling pulse beat high in me. My step was light on deck in the crisp air," he later wrote. "I felt that there could be no turning back, and that I was engaging in an adventure the meaning of which I thoroughly understood."

Slocum's voyage had all the elements of a classic sea adventure: narrowly escaping pirates off Gibraltar, a visit from the ghost of Columbus's pilot off the Canaries, and a terrifying four-day gale off Tierra del Fuego. By the time he sailed into Newport, three and a half years later, he had traveled 46,000 miles (85,000km) and become the first man to sail single handed around the world. No-one would repeat his feat until Louis Bernicot's circumnavigation of 1936–38— and by then the whole world had changed. But the genius of Slocum wasn't just to undertake such a journey but to write about it, and to write about it well. He had already penned two books about his previous adventures, and had a publishing deal for his next book in place before he even left Boston. *Around the World Alone* was duly published in 1900 and not only bought Slocum a farm in Martha's Vineyard, Massachusetts, but anchored him as one of the giants of ocean sailing. All thanks to an old Chesapeake Bay oyster dredger.

Centennial Republic

What better way to celebrate the USA's 100th birthday than to set off on a 2,600-mile (4,815km) trek down the Ohio and Mississippi Rivers in an all-American boat? In 1875, Nathaniel H. Bishop paddled from the ice of Pennsylvania to the warm waters of the Gulf of Mexico.

JOURNEY: Pittsburgh, Pennsylvania, to Suwannee River, Florida
BOAT NAME: *Centennial Republic*
CAPTAIN: Nathaniel H. Bishop
DATE: 1875–76
DISTANCE: 2,600 nautical miles (4,815km)

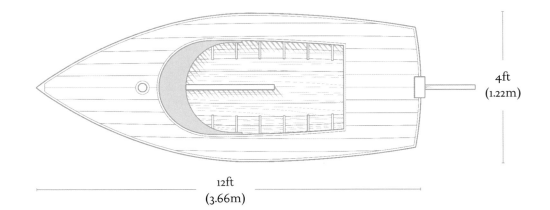

12ft
(3.66m)

4ft
(1.22m)

LENGTH: 12ft (3.66m)
BEAM: 4ft (1.22m)
MAX HEADROOM: 13in (33cm)
WEIGHT: 200lb (91kg)

DATE BUILT: 1875
RIG: Sprit
CREW: 1

2,600 *Miles in a Sneakbox*
Centennial Republic

★ ★ ★

THE UNITED STATES OF AMERICA was not quite 100 years old when in December 1875 Nathaniel H. Bishop set off alone from Pittsburgh, Pennsylvania in a small wooden boat. His journey was more modest than those of later, ocean-going adventurers but was remarkable in its own way. For Bishop planned to travel down the Ohio and Mississippi Rivers, along the coast of the Gulf of Mexico to Florida—a journey of some 2,600 miles (4,815km). His mode of transport was a mere nutshell of a boat, 12ft (3.66m) long by 4ft (1.22m) wide, which not only carried all his provisions and equipment but was his sleeping place for most of the voyage.

A tall, slight man who grew fruit for a living, Bishop clearly had a taste for adventure. Aged 17, he hitched a ride on a ship from Massachusetts to South America and then set off on a 1,000-mile (1,600km) walk around the continent, eventually crossing the Andes to the Pacific and hitching a ride home on a ship going around Cape Horn. Then in 1874, he set off from Quebec, Canada, in an 18ft (5.5m) canoe headed for the Gulf of Mexico, some 2,500 miles (4,630km) south. After 400 miles (741km), he sold his boat, which was too heavy, and completed the journey in a paper canoe weighing just 58lb (26.3kg).

Within a few months, Bishop was off again. This time, his vessel of choice was a sneakbox, a shallow, low-lying boat designed for hunting ducks—an unlikely choice for a 2,600-mile (4,200km) journey through fast-flowing water and across open sea. Bishop nevertheless paddled *Centennial Republic* downriver with the current, dodging ice floes until things warmed up further south. At night, he closed the hatch and slept in the 13in (33cm) deep hull, only occasionally resorting to shoreside lodgings. The account of his voyage, *Four Months in a Sneakbox* published in 1879, is a quietly captivating travelogue. For, as well as providing a scenic backdrop, the river was home to a teeming and sometimes scary subculture that Bishop had to negotiate. His descriptions of the cities he passed through (mainly Cincinnati and New Orleans) and the characters he met provide some of the most powerful passages in the book.

The sneakbox adventure was Bishop's last major trip, though he maintained his passion for small-boat cruising and in 1880 co-founded the American Canoe Association. *Four Months in a Sneakbox* became a classic and *Centennial Republic* was exhibited at the Smithsonian Institution.

Paratii

What is it about the polar regions that has so fascinated generations of explorers? Amyr Klink decided to find out for himself by mooring his boat in the ice for a year—alone. At the end of his long winter, a surprising thing happened that would turn his quiet retreat into a thrilling adventure.

JOURNEY: Paraty to Paraty, Brazil, via the Arctic and Antarctic
BOAT NAME: *Paratii*
CAPTAIN: Amyr Klink
DATE: 1989–91
DISTANCE: 27,000 nautical miles (50,000km)

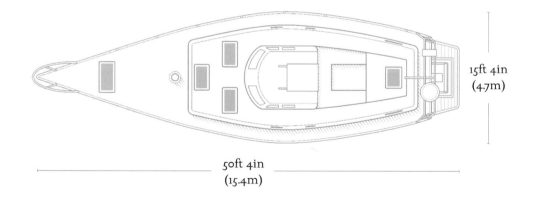

15ft 4in
(4.7m)

50ft 4in
(15.4m)

LENGTH: 50ft 4in (15.4m)
BEAM: 15ft 4in (4.7m)
DRAFT: 6ft (1.8m)
DISPLACEMENT: 22.4 tons (20.3 tonnes)

DATE BUILT: 1989
RIG: Cutter
CREW: 1

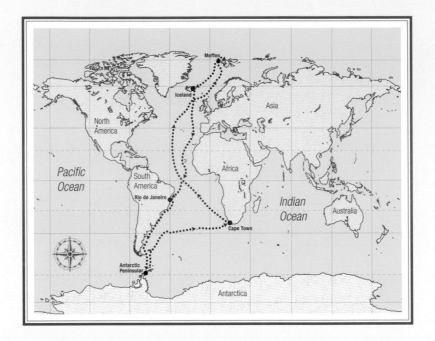

From Pole to Pole
Paratii

★ ★ ★

TO SPEND A YEAR IN THE ICE, alone, was Amyr Klink's wish. The Brazilian sailor had already made a name for himself when, in 1984, he became the first man to row across the South Atlantic: from Namibia to Brazil in 100 days. The journey gave him a taste for being alone at sea and fed his fascination with Antarctica and Shackleton's polar voyages. So he built himself a rugged aluminum cutter and packed it with enough stores to last him three and a half years—just in case. On New Year's Eve 1989, he headed south, and four weeks later moored up in Dorian Bay in Antarctica, due south of Cape Horn. And that was that. For the next year he went about his business, mostly with only the birds, penguins, and seals for company. *Paratii* was only the fourth yacht to have ever overwintered in Antarctica, and the first to do so solo. At one point, Klink went seven and a half months without seeing another human being, and grew increasingly fond of Barbara the Weddell seal, Theobald the sea elephant, and the countless gentoo penguins nesting close to his boat. He was anything but bored.

"In seven months, I couldn't remember two days the same," he wrote. "The snow, always different, the sea-ice now completely irregular, with strange, rounded forms trapped in it. Transformations were ceaseless; the volume of light, the colour of days, even the landscape."

At winter's end, he had a "Moitessian moment." Just like the French sailor in the Golden Globe Race of 1968 who decided to carry on sailing around the world rather than head back to "the snake pit," Klink decided he wasn't ready to go home yet. Instead, he sailed another 16,000 miles (29,600km) north to Spitsbergen in the Arctic Sea — sailing from 68° S to 80° N, traveling almost from Pole to Pole. His farthest point north was Moffen, an island where he spent just three hours before heading south again. It was a brief but halcyon moment. "Not because the island was so far from home, so high in latitude, so difficult to get to, but because for so long it was the place I had dreamed of reaching. Moffen had become the summit of a long and beautiful escalator."

Klink arrived back in Brazil in October 1991, nearly two years after he'd set off, and started planning his next voyage: a solo circumnavigation of Antarctica, which he successfully completed in 1998. He detailed his time in the Antarctic in his book, *Between Two Poles*.

Swallow

*W*HEN *A*RTHUR *R*ANSOME WROTE AN UNASSUMING BOOK ABOUT THE ADVENTURES OF A BUNCH
OF CHILDREN ON A COUPLE OF BOATS ON AN *E*NGLISH LAKE, HE CAN'T HAVE IMAGINED IT WOULD
APPEAL TO A SECRET LONGING IN MILLIONS OF PEOPLE—ADULTS AND CHILDREN ALIKE.

ROUTE: Fictional lake, based on Coniston Water, UK
BOAT NAME: *Swallow*
CAPTAIN: John Walker
DATE: 1929
DISTANCE: Half a nautical mile (1km)

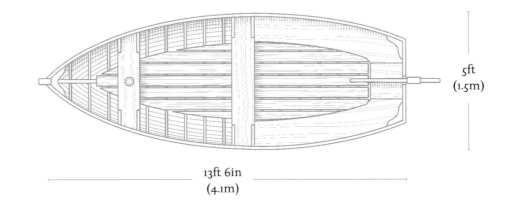

5ft
(1.5m)

13ft 6in
(4.1m)

LENGTH: 13ft 6in (4.1m) DATE BUILT: *ca.*1912
BEAM: 5ft (1.5m) RIG: Lug
DRAFT: 8 in (0.2m) CREW: 4
DISPLACEMENT: 250lb (114kg)

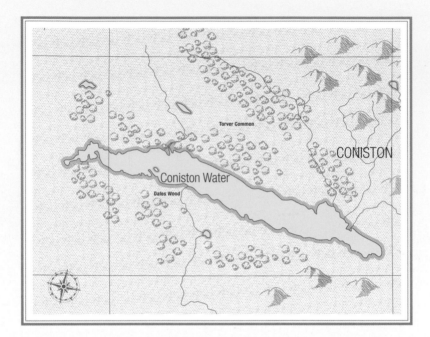

Within the map: Torver Common · CONISTON · Coniston Water · Dales Wood

Swallows and Amazons Forever!
Swallow

★ ★ ★

IT DOESN'T SOUND LIKE THE most exciting storyline: a group of children messing about in boats on a fictional lake, based on Coniston Water in England, pestering an uncle who's trying to write a book on a houseboat moored nearby. Hardly the makings of a Hollywood blockbuster. Yet Arthur Ransome's 1930 book *Swallows and Amazons* not only spawned a series of bestselling books and several TV, film, stage, and radio adaptations, but has become a catchphrase for a whole type of sailing experience. When someone says they're going on a "Swallows and Amazons adventure," we know immediately what they mean.

Ransome based the story of the six children—John, Susan, Titty, and Roger Walker in a dinghy named *Swallow*, and Nancy and Peggy Blackett in another called *Amazon*—on a summer he spent in the Lake District teaching his friends' children to sail. Both boats were quintessential wooden sailing dinghies of the era: built from wood, with traditional clinker planking and lug-rigged sails. Ransome wrote that *Swallow* was "a fast little boat and a steady little boat, in fact the best little boat that ever was built," while *Amazon* was "a fine little ship, with varnished pine planking. She was a much newer boat than the *Swallow*, of the same length, but not quite so roomy."

The adventures that followed tapped into a common longing for free, unfettered adventure: away from home, school, and grownups—though always safe and squeaky clean. By grafting the children's pirate fantasy onto an idyllic English landscape, Ransome managed to splice together romantic ideas of the sea, childish innocence, and an idealized view of nature, so that by the end of the book the reader can't help but shout, "Swallows and Amazons forever!"

At the end of the summer of 1929, Ransome took over ownership of *Swallow*, while the Altounyans kept *Mavis* (*Amazon*). Ransome owned *Swallow* until 1935, when he sold her to Roger Fothergill, a local boy aged about 15. After making a few alterations to improve her sailing performance, Fothergill took the boat to Morecambe Bay where he enjoyed his own adventures, sleeping under an awning and cooking on a camping stove. He sold *Swallow* in 1939, and her fate after that is unknown. *Mavis/Amazon*, meanwhile, was restored in 1989 and loaned to the Windermere Steamboat Museum, where she is still on display.

Mazurek

With most of the men's sailing records already set, in the mid-1970s the spotlight turned on the women. Polish naval engineer Krystyna Chojnowska-Liskiewicz was determined to be the first woman to sail around the world solo—so why is her record so often ignored in favor of her Anglophonic rival?

JOURNEY: Las Palmas to Las Palmas, Canary Islands, via the world
BOAT NAME: *Mazurek*
CAPTAIN: Krystyna Chojnowska-Liskiewicz
DATE: 1976–78
DISTANCE: 31,166 nautical miles (57,720km)

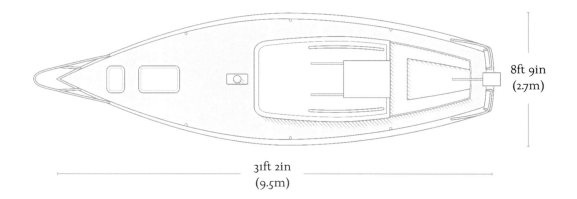

8ft 9in
(2.7m)

31ft 2in
(9.5m)

LENGTH: 31ft 2in (9.5m)
BEAM: 8ft 9in (2.7m)
DRAFT: 3ft (1m)
DISPLACEMENT: 6 tons (6.1 tonnes)

DATE BUILT: 1975
RIG: Sloop
CREW: 1

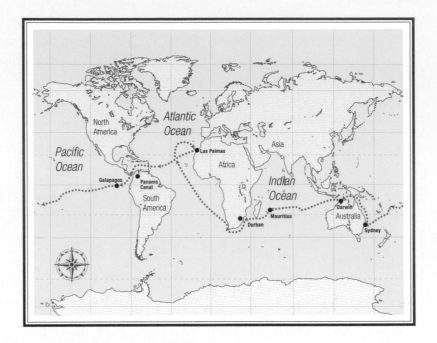

East vs West

Mazurek

★ ★ ★

THE COLD WAR WAS IN FULL SWING when Krystyna Chojnowska-Liskiewicz set off from Las Palmas in her attempt to become the first woman to sail around the world single-handed. It was seven years since Robin Knox-Johnson had done it for the men (nonstop), and at least three other women were limbering up to win the prize for the West. For Chojnowska-

Liskiewicz, a naval engineer with extensive sailing experience, it was a matter of national pride that she should claim the record for Poland. So much so that her whole voyage was funded by the Polish Yachting Association, who gave her intensive training and arranged for her boat to be transported to Las Palmas to give her the best possible start.

The patriotic Pole set off in March 1976, sailing across the Atlantic to the Caribbean and then through the Panama Canal, which offered a safer route into the Pacific than the dreaded Cape Horn. It was a decision that would cost her the record in many people's eyes. Like Robin Lee Graham a decade before (who also sailed via the Panama Canal), the Polish sailor received extensive outside support (in her case, from the Polish Navy) and had frequent stops (19 in all) during her long circumnavigation of the globe. Things began to heat up, however, with the news that two other women were also attempting to claim the honor— New Zealand sailor Naomi James and Brigitte Oudry from France. The last leg of Chojnowska-Liskiewicz's journey became a genuine race, not just between her and the other two women, but between East and West, communism and capitalism.

In the end, Chojnowska-Liskiewicz made it back to Las Palmas in April 1978, after 401 days, and easily claimed the record. She was followed six weeks later by James, who completed her loop in just 272 days, beating Francis Chichester's time by two days. Back in Poland, Chojnowska-Liskiewicz was welcomed as a national hero, but her achievements went largely unnoticed in the West, which was too busy celebrating the return of James. There were many who felt the Polish sailor had cheated by sailing via the Panama Canal and receiving so much outside assistance, and that the record should rightfully go to the New Zealander, who had sailed via Cape Horn. With the benefit of hindsight, it's hard not to think there was an element of Cold War politics in play. With the collapse of the Eastern Bloc and the advent of the internet, however, Chojnowska-Liskiewicz is finally getting the recognition she deserves.

Super Silver

IN THE SAME YEAR THAT NEIL ARMSTRONG BECAME THE FIRST MAN TO STEP ON THE MOON AND ROBIN KNOX-JOHNSTON BECAME THE FIRST MAN TO SAIL AROUND THE WORLD SOLO AND NONSTOP, TWO MEN WERE FIGHTING ANOTHER BATTLE: TO BE THE FIRST TO ROW SOLO ACROSS THE ATLANTIC

JOURNEY: St John's, Newfoundland, to Blacksod Bay, Ireland
BOAT NAME: *Super Silver*
CAPTAIN: Tom McClean
DATE: 1969
DISTANCE: 1,885 nautical miles (3,490km)

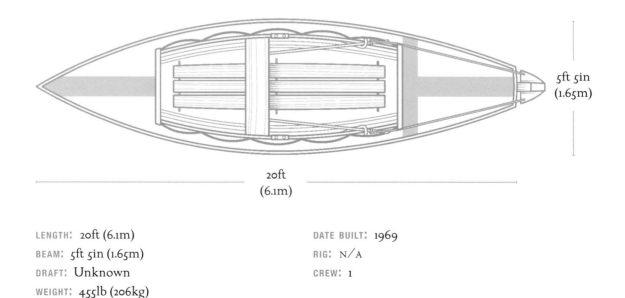

5ft 5in
(1.65m)

20ft
(6.1m)

LENGTH: 20ft (6.1m)
BEAM: 5ft 5in (1.65m)
DRAFT: Unknown
WEIGHT: 455lb (206kg)

DATE BUILT: 1969
RIG: N/A
CREW: 1

30

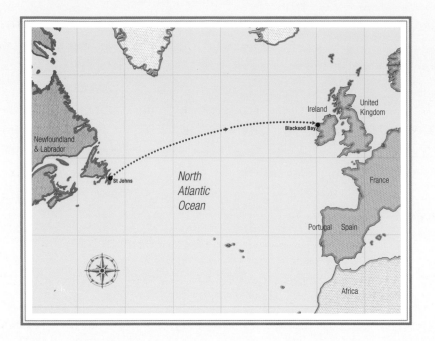

Race Across the Atlantic
Super Silver

★ ★ ★

TOM MCCLEAN WAS ALREADY FIGHTING against the odds when he set off to become the first person to row solo across the Atlantic on May 17, 1969. His rival John Fairfax had left the Canaries four months earlier and was already halfway to America. McClean had one last trick up his sleeve: rather than row the warm, 4,500-mile-(8,300km-) long southern route, he opted for the cold northern route, from Newfoundland to Ireland, cutting nearly 2,500 miles (4,600km) off the journey—providing he survived gales and extreme cold. Even taking this shorter route into account, Fairfax was still well ahead and rowing in favorable conditions.

It was the sort of challenge McClean relished. Brought up in an orphanage where until the age of 15 he was known simply as number "81," he was in the Parachute Regiment for six years before joining the Special Air Service. When he heard that two officers from his former platoon, John Ridgway and Chay Blyth, were attempting to row the Atlantic, he was immediately mesmerized by the idea and determined to do the same, but alone. Trouble was, Fairfax had had the same idea.

The two men's choice of boat was strikingly different. While Fairfax had chosen a modern design by the renowned dinghy designer Uffa Fox, McClean chose a traditional dory of the type that had been used by fishermen on the Grand Banks for centuries. *Super Silver* was adapted to her new role with a raised deck fore and aft to provide shelter from the elements and buoyancy in case of capsize, but otherwise the hull shape was essentially unchanged.

After an eventful crossing, including capsizing 600 miles (1,100km) from home, he landed in Ireland on July 26—only to discover Fairfax had beaten him by eight days. McClean could, however, claim the record for the fastest crossing—70 days compared to Fairfax's 180—and was the first man to row across solo from west to east. He went on to set another record in 1982, when he sailed the smallest boat to cross the Atlantic, the 9ft 9in (2.97m) *Giltspur*. When his record was broken three weeks later by someone sailing a boat 8in (20cm) shorter than his, he took a chainsaw and chopped 2ft (60cm) off *Giltspur* to reclaim the record. Likewise, when his Atlantic rowing record was broken, he returned with *Super Silver* (renamed *Skol 1080*) and reclaimed it with a time of 54 days—a record that remains unbroken to this day.

Nova Espero

Colin and Stanley Smith took self-promotion to a new level when they sailed a 20ft (6.1m) open boat across the Atlantic to publicize their boatbuilding skills. Their verdict at the end of the 43-day crossing? "We've just about had enough!"

JOURNEY: Dartmouth, Nova Scotia, to Dartmouth, UK
BOAT NAME: *Nova Espero*
CAPTAIN: Colin and Stanley Smith
DATE: 1949
DISTANCE: 3,000 nautical miles (5,550m)

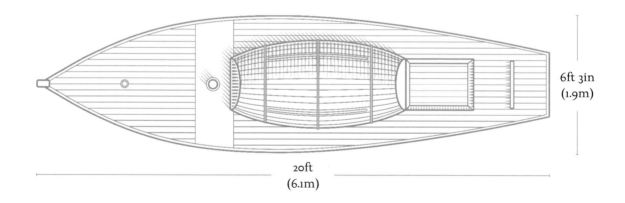

6ft 3in
(1.9m)

20ft
(6.1m)

LENGTH: 20ft (6.1m)
BEAM: 6ft 3in (1.9m)
DRAFT: 2ft 10in (86cm)
DISPLACEMENT: 1.5 tons (1.36 tonnes)

DATE BUILT: 1949
RIG: Sloop (later yawl)
CREW: 2

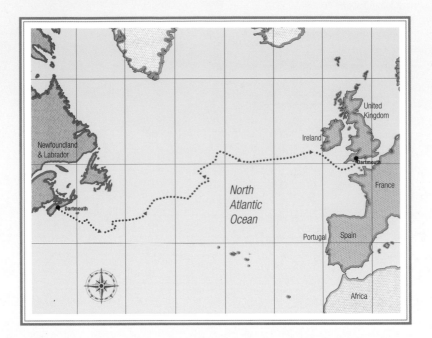

15-Minute Heroes
Nova Espero

★ ★ ★

WHEN COLIN AND STANLEY SMITH set off for Canada to set up a boatyard in 1949, they needed a way to prove their credentials to potential clients. The plan they came up with was simple: they would build a boat in Canada and sail it across the Atlantic and back. The only catch was, that they could only afford to build a very small boat.

Having worked in the design office at the Saunders-Roe boatyard, Colin and Stanley knew about boat design, and as they headed across the Atlantic on RMS *Aquitania*, the pair designed their vessel: a 20ft (6.1m) clinker-built sailing boat, with a simple sloop rig and no cabin. It was ideal for a day sailing off the coast of England, but hardly suitable for an ocean voyage. The brothers nevertheless built the boat in a damp cellar in Halifax, along with a 7ft (2.1m) long dinghy that they lashed over the cockpit to make a roof. That gave them 3ft 6in (1.06m) headroom. There weren't any bunks, so the brothers took turns sleeping on the cabin sole. They couldn't afford to buy a chronometer, log, barometer, or oilskins, but navigated using a simple compass and sextant. The boat was called *Nova Espero*: Esperanto for "new hope."

The Smith brothers set of from Dartmouth, Nova Scotia, on July 6, 1949, and, close encounters with whales notwithstanding, seem to have had a mostly miserable time. Halfway across, Colin fell over the side and was saved only because Stanley happened to see him going over. By the time they reached Ireland, their supplies were down to three biscuits, a few potatoes, and a pinch of sugar. They arrived in Dartmouth, UK, on August 18 after 43 days at sea, to be greeted by the Royal Navy, a fleet of yachts, and enormous crowds cheering from the shore. As the local paper put it: "The Smith boys from Devon [...] have become the heroes of Britain overnight." Or as Stanley put it: "We learned this thing about the voyage: it's not a good thing to make a habit of crossing the North Atlantic in a 20-foot boat. We've just about had enough."

Nova Espero was subsequently exhibited at the Festival of Britain in 1951. The brothers had succeeded in getting the publicity they needed, but their planned business venture was not to be. Colin got married and settled in Britain, while Stanley sailed *Nova Espero* to New York with Charles Violet in 1951. This time the boat had a proper cabin and an improved rig. Back home in England, Stanley designed a new boat: the 14ft (4.27m) West Wight Potter, which went on to develop a cult following and brought "new hope" to thousands of sailors.

Huck's raft

*It's just a **16ft** by **16ft** (5m by 5m) stack of planks with wooden pegs, but Huck's raft has come to symbolize so much more; human relations, freedom, growing up, and our relationship with nature. In short, nothing less than the human condition.*

JOURNEY: St Petersburg, Missouri, to Pikesville, Arkansas (both fictional locations)
BOAT NAME: Unnamed
CAPTAINS: Huckleberry Finn and Jim
DATE: 1884
DISTANCE: 1,100 nautical miles (2,037km)

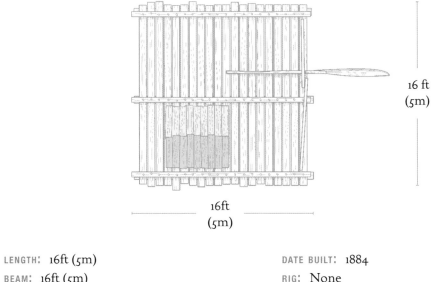

16 ft
(5m)

16ft
(5m)

LENGTH: 16ft (5m)

BEAM: 16ft (5m)

DRAFT: 12in (30cm)

WEIGHT: Unknown

DATE BUILT: 1884

RIG: None

CREW: 2

Raft of Hope
Huck's raft

★ ★ ★

IT'S NO SECRET THAT BOATS are symbols of freedom, the means of escape from the stultifying confines of conventional society. They are the holders of our dreams, which will transport us away from the petty worries of everyday life to a truer and more noble version of ourselves. But what about a lone raft set adrift on a river, with no means of propulsion?

It is hardly the most inspiring vessel on which to set a life-or-death adventure. Yet that is what Mark Twain does in his renowned 1884 novel *Adventures of Huckleberry Finn*. And what a potent symbol it turns out to be. There have been reams written about the symbolism of the Mississippi River, as the liminal place where Huck and Jim can forge their friendship irrespective of their age or race, as well as the simple raft that carries them over it. Indeed, it almost seems as if the very soul of the nation is bound up in that pile of pegged-together wooden planks.

Having famously worked for several years as a pilot on the Mississippi, Twain not only knew its currents and shallows intimately but also the types of craft that navigated on it. Huck's raft is therefore likely to be closely based on fact. And indeed there were just such rafts of timber lashed together and floating downriver to the sawmills. Most of these were several hundred feet long but were made of sections, or "cribs," about 16ft (5m) wide by 16ft (5m) long, which could become detached during their long journey south. It's one of these sections, it seems, that Huck and Jim find and proceed to turn into their floating home, with the addition of a small "wigwam" made of planks with a firebox inside to prevent the flames being spotted by unwelcome eyes. For both of them are on the run: Huck from the physical abuse meted out by his father and the "sivilizing" ways of Widow Douglas, and Jim from the chains of slavery.

The result is a no-man's-land (the raft) propelled by the elemental forces of nature (the river) and set apart from the rest of society (the shore). You don't have to work too hard to read meaning into this: "I was power glad to get away from the feuds, and so was Jim to get away from the swamp. We said there warn't no home like a raft, after all. Other places do seem so cramped up and smothery, but a raft don't. You feel mighty free and easy and comfortable on a raft."

Suhaili

It was billed as the race of the century: to be the first person to sail around the world single-handed and nonstop. Nine boats started, but only one finished—and it wasn't the fastest or biggest or most expensive yacht that won. Far from it...

JOURNEY: Falmouth to Falmouth, UK, via the world
BOAT NAME: *Suhaili*
CAPTAIN: Robin Knox-Johnston
DATE: 1968–69
DISTANCE: 30,000 nautical miles (55,500km)

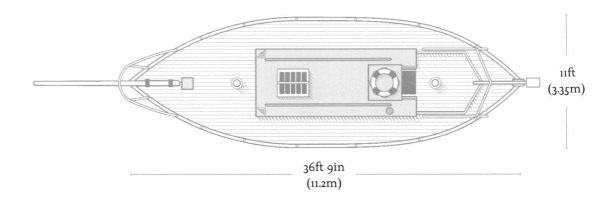

11ft
(3.35m)

36ft 9in
(11.2m)

LENGTH: 32ft (9.75m)
BEAM: 11ft (3.35m)
DRAFT: 5ft (1.5m)
DISPLACEMENT: 7.04 tons (6.39 tonnes)

DATE BUILT: 1964
RIG: Ketch
CREW: 1

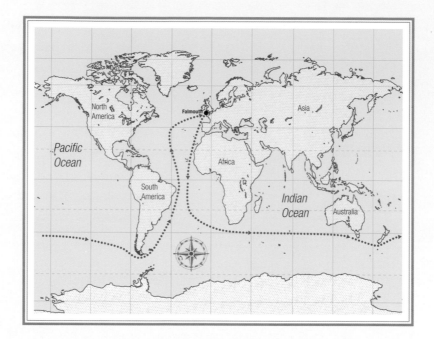

Loop the Loop
Suhaili

★ ★ ★

FRANCIS CHICHESTER HAD BARELY MADE IT safely home to the UK before the chatter started. By sailing around the world single-handed in a record-breaking 226 days, with just one stop in Australia, Chichester had shown what could be done. The only question now was who would be the first to make the same journey *without stopping*? The challenge was formalized in March 1968 when *The Sunday Times* offered two prizes: the Golden Globe trophy for the first person to loop the loop, and £5,000 for the person to do it in the fastest time. The only requirement was that competitors should start their journeys from a British port between June 1 and October 31, 1968.

Robin Knox-Johnston was a British Merchant Navy officer with a strong patriotic streak. He and some friends had built a 32ft (9.75m) wooden ketch called *Suhaili* in India a few years earlier and he had sailed her 10,000 miles (18,500km) from South Africa to England on his own. He was determined the winner should be British and, not being able to secure enough sponsorship to build a new boat, decided to set out on the slow but sturdy *Suhaili*. Setting off on June 14, he was the third competitor to start. Nine boats would eventually enter the race, of which four never made it out of the Atlantic and another retired after rounding the Cape of Good Hope. Of the remainder, Donald Crowhurst faked a round-the world-voyage while pottering around the Atlantic before apparently committing suicide, Nigel Tetley's boat sank just 1,100 miles (2,000km) from the finish, while Bernard Moitessier opted out of the race and sailed on to Tahiti instead.

Only the unflappable Robin Knox-Johnston carried on regardless, despite sailing one of the slowest boats in the race, suffering several knockdowns and losing the use of both his radio and his self-steering gear. He eventually made it back into Falmouth on April 22, 1969, after 313 days at sea—thereby winning both the Golden Globe and the £5,000 cash prize (which he promptly donated to Crowhurst's widow). *Suhaili* was subsequently exhibited at the National Maritime Museum in London and undertook two more major voyages: across the Atlantic using historic navigation instruments in 1989 and then to Greenland in 1991. Meanwhile, Sir Robin proved that age was no barrier to adventure when he entered the 2006 Velux 5 Oceans round-the-world race at the age of 67. He finished a close fourth—out of four finishers.

Sea Serpent

It was the maddest race: 3,000 miles (5,550km) across the Atlantic in 15ft (4.6m) boats, solo and unassisted. The prize: $3,000 and the record for being the smallest boat to cross the Atlantic—until the next maniac set off in the next smallest boat...

ROUTE: Boston, Massachusetts, to Cornwall, UK
BOAT NAME: *Sea Serpent*
CAPTAIN: Josiah Lawlor
DATE: 1891
DISTANCE: 3,000 nautical miles (5,550km)

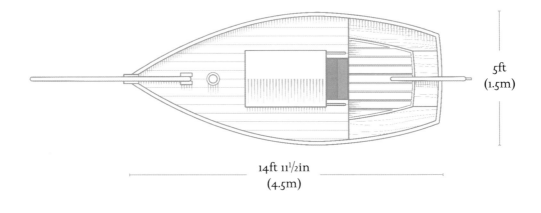

5ft
(1.5m)

14ft 11½in
(4.5m)

LENGTH: 14ft 11½in (4.5m)
BEAM: 5ft (1.5m)
DEPTH OF HULL: 2ft (60cm)
DISPLACEMENT: Unknown

DATE BUILT: 1891
RIG: Sloop
CREW: 1

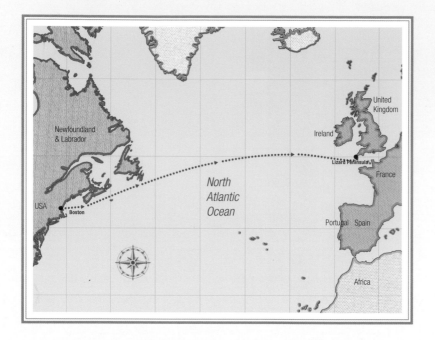

The Tale of the Hungry Shark
Sea Serpent

★ ★ ★

IT ALL STARTED BACK IN 1866, when J.M. Hudson and F.E. Fitch crossed the Atlantic from west to east, from New York to Margate, England, on a 26ft (7.9m) lifeboat. Four years later, they were "beaten" by J.C. Thomas and Nikola Primorac, who crossed from east to west, from Cork, Ireland to Boston, Massachusetts, on a 20ft (6.1m) boat. They in turn were then "beaten" by Alfred Johnson, who crossed from west to east, from New Brunswick, Canada to Albertcastle, England, also on a 20ft (6.1m) boat, but single-handed. And so it went on, as the competition for the smallest boat to cross the Atlantic intensified and the boats got smaller, and smaller, and smaller. By 1891, it was the turn of William Andrews—who had already set a transatlantic record in a 19-footer (5.8m) with his brother Asa—to attempt a single-handed crossing with a 15ft (4.5m) boat called *Mermaid*. When he discovered Josiah Lawlor was doing the same with his 15ft (4.5m) dory *Sea Serpent*, the pair decided to turn it into a race. The prize was a silver cup and $3,000 in cash.

The two boats set sail from the Ocean Pier, near Boston, Massachusetts, in the early hours of June 17, 1981, in front of 25,000 well-wishers. Both men had eventful crossings, including being capsized several times and having to bail their boats out in mid-ocean. Both had several encounters with sharks, although Lawlor came up with the most ingenious solution when one of the animals started chewing his keel: he wrapped a flare in a newspaper and threw it over the side where it exploded in the jaws of the hungry predator. He was never bothered by that particular shark again. In the end, it was Lawlor who made it across to the Lizard Peninsula, UK, in just 45 days, while Andrews had to be rescued by a passing ship. Lawlor's log of the voyage ended with these words of advice for aspiring sailors: "Don't go to sea, boys."

Despite his own warning, the following year Lawlor attempted the crossing again in a slightly smaller boat, the 14ft 6in (4.4m) *Christopher Columbus*. He and his boat were never seen again. Andrews, meanwhile, sailed again a few weeks after Lawlor in his 14ft 6in (4.4m) *Sapolio* and set a record that would stand for 73 years. Still not satisfied, he tried twice more in even smaller boats, but failed both times. Finally, in 1901, he set off on a transatlantic honeymoon with his new bride on board a boat called the *Flying Dutchman*. Neither they nor their boat were ever seen again.

Pride of the Thames

The story of three men cavorting in a boat on the Thames shocked the English establishment when it was published in 1889 (they thought it was vulgar), but it soon became a publishing sensation and has gone on to become a comic classic.

JOURNEY: Kingston to Oxford; Oxford to Pangbourne, UK
BOAT NAME: *Pride of the Thames*
CAPTAIN: Jerome K. Jerome
DATE: 1889
DISTANCE: 120 nautical miles (193km)

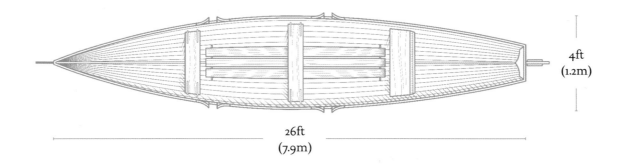

4ft
(1.2m)

26ft
(7.9m)

LENGTH: 26ft (7.9m)
BEAM: 4ft (1.2m)
DRAFT: 8in (20cm)
WEIGHT: 120lb (54kg)

DATE BUILT: 1840s
RIG: N/A
CREW: 3

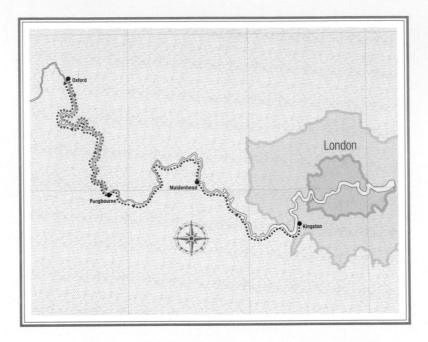

Three Men in a Boat
The Pride of the Thames

★ ★ ★

PLEASURE BOATING ON THE THAMES enjoyed a sudden burst of popularity at the end of the nineteenth century, with rowing skiffs, slipper launches, and even the occasional gondola thronging the waters between London and Oxford. In peak season, some 800 boats a day passed through Boulter's Lock near Maidenhead. It was a perfect time to write a travel guide to navigating the Upper Thames, which is what Jerome K. Jerome set out to do in 1889, having enjoyed a pleasant honeymoon on the river. Somewhere along the way, however, his serious intention was hijacked by comic wit, as he described a two-week vacation with his friends George (real name George Wingrave) and Harry (real name Carl Hentschel), and their (fictional) dog Montmorency. As his creative juices flowed, the travel guide became relegated to a few sections of slightly purplish prose, which most readers skipped to get to the "funny bits."

The result is one of the funniest and most successful books ever written: continuously in print since it was first published in 1889, adapted to TV and film at least half a dozen times, and regularly featured in lists of top books to this day. One classic scene takes place in Chapter 12, when the three men attempt to open a can of pineapple without a can opener. They sustain various injuries using a variety of tools, including the boat's mast, before throwing the tin in the river and rowing off in disgust. Without missing a beat, Jerome carries straight on with his next comic scene: "Maidenhead itself is too snobby to be pleasant. It is the haunt of the river swell and his overdressed female companion. It is the town of showy hotels, patronised chiefly by dudes and ballet girls." By this time, his supposed travel guide has descended (or ascended?) to outright farce.

The trio travel on two hire boats: one for the journey from Kingston up to Oxford, the other for the journey back. Both are two-man skiffs, around 26ft (7.9m) long, and based on the type of boats used as taxis on the Thames for hundreds of years. Their first boat barely warrants a description, but the second becomes the butt of Jerome's ire, as the friends argue about whether the so-called *Pride of the Thames* is a Roman relic or the fossil of a prehistoric whale. Eventually, they set off again: "We fastened the so-called boat together with some pieces of string, got a bit of wall-paper and pasted over the shabbier places, said our prayers, and stepped on board." Riverboating has never been so much fun.

Dorade

No one was surprised when the legendary Dorade won a string of classic yacht regattas after being restored in 1997. But a 2,250-mile (4,200km) ocean race against some of the most modern yachts in the world? Surely, that was just plain daft...

JOURNEY: Los Angeles, California to Honolulu, Hawai'i
BOAT NAME: *Dorade*
CAPTAIN: Olin Stephens and Matt Brooks
DATE: 1936 and 2013
DISTANCE: 2,250 nautical miles (4,200km)

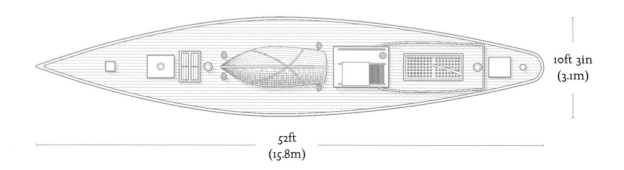

10ft 3in
(3.1m)

52ft
(15.8m)

LENGTH: 52ft (15.8m)
BEAM: 10ft 3in (3.1m)
DRAFT: 7ft 7in (2.3m)
DISPLACEMENT: 16.5 tons (15 tonnes)

DATE BUILT: 1929–30
RIG: Yawl
CREW: 7

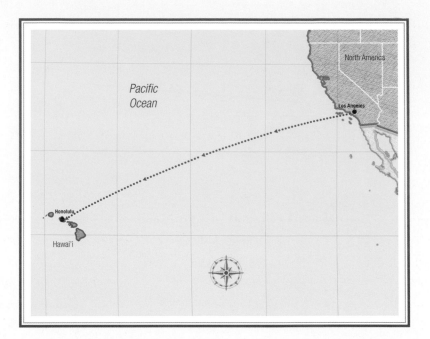

Pacific
Ocean

North America

Los Angeles

Honolulu

Hawai'i

Once a Winner...
Dorade

★ ★ ★

IT WAS A CRAZY IDEA, to race an 83-year-old classic yacht against a fleet of ultramodern speedsters, pitting wood against carbon fiber, bronze against Spectra™. And as *Dorade* headed out of Los Angeles to race 2,250 miles (4,200km) in the biannual Transpacific Yacht Race, there were some who accused her owners of putting an irreplaceable piece of maritime history unnecessarily at risk. After all, there was no way this floating antique was going to beat any of the modern boats, let alone win the race, so why bother? Yet, when *Dorade* stormed into Honolulu 12 days, 5 hours and 23 minutes later, she had not only knocked more than a day off her previous time but had the fastest overall time on handicap. Seventy-seven years after her 1936 triumph, *Dorade* had won the race again. It was an astonishing result that made headlines around the world, even in such normally disinterested papers such as *The New York Times.*

Dorade was the first major commission for a promising young designer called Olin Stephens, who was just 21 when he drew her. With her slim hull and lightweight construction, "Design No./" was a radical departure from the heavy schooners that dominated ocean racing at the time. Yet, in her first major test, the 1931 Transatlantic Race, *Dorade* finished two days ahead of her much larger rivals. She went on to win the Fastnet Race that year and, when Olin and his crew returned to New York a few weeks later, they were given a ticker-tape parade through the city. *Dorade* continued her winning ways, coming first in the Bermuda Race in 1932 and the Fastnet Race again in 1933, before beating all-comers in the 1936 Transpac. Her success and that of her near-sistership *Stormy Weather* launched the fledgling firm of Sparkman & Stephens, which would go on to produce a string of successful designs, including six America's Cup winners. By the time he retired in 1978, Olin Stephens had created more than 2,000 designs.

Dorade's place in yachting history was already firmly established by the time she was restored in 1997, and a life gracing various classic-yacht regattas seemed assured—until Matt Brooks and his wife Pam Rorke Levy bought her in 2010. Inspired by her history, they set out on a campaign to revisit all the races she had won in her heyday, starting with the 2013 Transpac. That was followed by the 2014 Newport Bermuda Race (1st in class), the 2015 Transatlantic (2nd in class), and the 2015 Fastnet (2nd in class). Whatever next?

Casanova's gondola

Casanova is mostly remembered for one thing only—his powers of seduction—but he led a rich life full of adventure, including his escape from an "inescapable" prison at the heart of Venice. His means of escape? A gondola, of course.

ROUTE: Doge's Palace to Mestre, Venice
BOAT NAME: Unnamed
CAPTAIN: Unknown
DATE: 1757
DISTANCE: 5.5 nautical miles (8.85km)

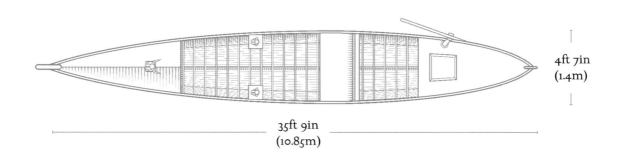

4ft 7in
(1.4m)

35ft 9in
(10.85m)

LENGTH: 35ft 7in (10.85m)
BEAM: 4ft 7in (1.4m)
DRAFT: Shallow
DISPLACEMENT: 770lb (350kg)

DATE BUILT: Unknown
RIG: N/A
CREW: 4

Casanova's Escape
Casanova's gondola

★ ★ ★

AS ESCAPES GO, it was hardly the most daring or even the most dangerous, even if Piombi prison in the Doge's Palace was known to be inescapable, but Casanova's breakout features many of the key ingredients to make up a classic Italian tale: a Venetian palace, a fat monk, gondolas, and, of course, pasta.

Born in Venice in 1725, Giacomo Casanova studied for the priesthood before embarking on a life of gambling and general debauchery. One of his favorite tricks as a young man was to untie the mooring lines on the gondolas and watch the ensuing chaos as their owners tried to retrieve them. He traveled widely across Europe, seducing women at every turn, before returning to Venice in 1753 to start a career as a magician. But two years later he was arrested for "public outrages against the holy church" and sentenced to five years' imprisonment. Inevitably, perhaps, his transport to the Piombi prison, under the roof of the Doge's Palace, was by gondola. After months of solitary confinement, he teamed up with a fellow prisoner, Father Balbi, to plan their escape. According to Casanova's biography, he smuggled a steel spike to Balbi by hiding it in a Bible under a large platter of macaroni cheese. Finally, at midnight on October 31, 1756, Casanova broke through the roof of the Doge's Palace and, Father Balbi clutching at his waist, managed to work his way into the main part of the building.

The pair were released the following morning by unsuspecting guards who thought they had been locked in overnight. Casanova immediately summoned a two-man gondola to take them to Mestre, on the mainland, where they later hired a coach and horses to take them "beyond the borders of the Republic." As they made their way out of Venice, Casanova looked back at the canals of his homeland. "It was a glorious morning, the air was clear and glowing with the first rays of the sun, and my two young watermen rowed easily and well; and as I thought over the night of sorrow, the dangers I had escaped, the abode where I had been fast bound the day before, all the chances which had been in my favor, and the liberty of which I now began to taste the sweets, I was so moved in my heart and grateful to my God that, well nigh choked with emotion, I burst into tears."

Casanova wouldn't return to Venice—and his beloved gondolas—for another 18 years, by which time he had led a life rich in travel, intrigue, and sex.

Megan Jaye

Six months before he died, John Lennon fulfilled a long-held ambition to go sailing—and not just on a family cruise, but a serious ocean passage in serious ocean weather. The result was a life-changing adventure that inspired his last album.

ROUTE: Newport, Rhode Island, to Bermuda
BOAT NAME: *Megan Jaye*
CAPTAIN: Hank Halsted
DATE: 1980
DISTANCE: 635 nautical miles (1,176km)

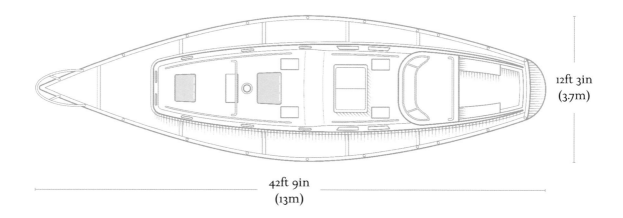

12ft 3in
(3.7m)

42ft 9in
(13m)

LENGTH: 42ft 9in (13m)
BEAM: 12ft 3in (3.7m)
DRAFT: 4ft 3in (1.3m)/11ft 6in (3.5m)
(centerboard down)

DISPLACEMENT: 11.8 tons (10.7 tonnes)
DATE BUILT: 1977
RIG: Sloop
CREW: 5

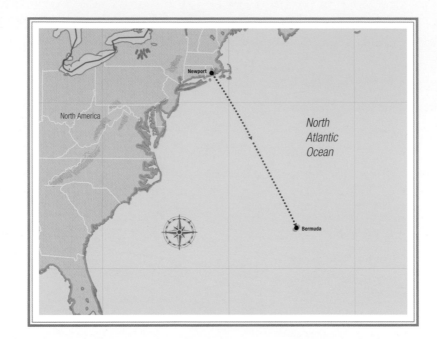

Lennon's Ocean Fantasy

Megan Jaye

★ ★ ★

DESPITE BEING ONE OF THE most successful musicians on the planet, by the spring of 1980 John Lennon had lost his mojo. The solution, according to Lennon's and Yoko Ono's spiritual adviser Takashi Yoshikawa, was to head southeast to escape the clouds casting shadows over his life. So Lennon flew to Newport, Rhode Island, and hired a boat. Lennon's father had been a merchant seaman, and he had long dreamed of going on a sea voyage. More importantly, according to Yoshikawa, the stars were in the correct alignment for such a voyage.

The boat Lennon chartered was a 43ft (13m) sloop called *Megan Jaye*, skippered by Hank Halsted. The destination was Bermuda, 635 miles (1,176 km) southeast of Newport. The only other people on board were Tyler Coneys, Lennon's new sailing buddy from New York, and Coneys's two cousins. After setting off from Newport on June 4, 1980, the five enjoyed two days of idyllic sailing, with bright sunshine and dolphins playing off the boat's bow. As the least experienced crew, Lennon was in charge of the galley and shared a watch with Tyler. On the third day, the boat was hit by a storm, with 60-knot (110km/h) winds and 20ft (6m) waves. The crew struggled with seasickness—apart from Lennon and Halsted, and after 48 hours at the helm, Halsted was exhausted and, despite the conditions, handed over to Lennon.

"At first you panic, and then you're ready to throw up your guts," Lennon recalled later. "But once you got out there and start doing all the stuff, you forget your fears and you got high on your performance. Once I accepted the reality of the situation, something greater than me took over and all of a sudden I lost my fear. I actually began to enjoy the experience and I started to shout out old sea shanties in the face of the storm, screaming at the thundering sky."

Megan Jaye arrived safely in Bermuda seven days later. Lennon, brimming with confidence, had rediscovered his mojo. "I was so centered after the experience at sea," he said. "All these songs came. After five years of nothing, no inspiration, no thought, no anything, then suddenly voom voom voom." The result was the album *Double Fantasy*, released in November 1980.

Three weeks later, Lennon was dead, shot by a deranged fan. As he wrote: "Life is what happens to you when you're busy making other plans."

Arabia

THE FELUCCA HAS BEEN A COMMON SIGHT ON THE RIVER NILE SINCE TIME IMMEMORIAL.
WILLARD PRICE, AUTHOR, ADVENTURER, AND POSSIBLE AMERICAN SPY, CHARTERED ONE TO
EXPLORE TRADITIONAL VILLAGE LIFE ALONG THE RIVER'S BANKS, UNTIL HE CAPSIZED. . .

JOURNEY: Aswan to Cairo, Egypt
BOAT NAME: *Arabia*
CAPTAIN: Willard Price
DATE: 1939
JOURNEY DISTANCE: 600 nautical miles (1,100km)

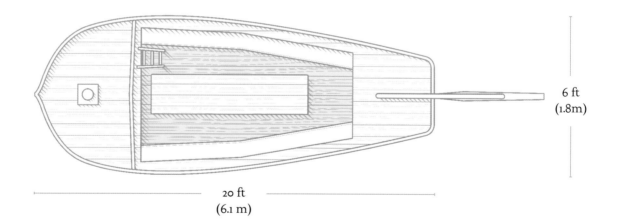

20 ft
(6.1 m)

6 ft
(1.8m)

LENGTH: 20ft (6.1m)

BEAM: 6ft (1.8m)

DRAFT: 1ft 6in (0.45m)

DISPLACEMENT: 8 tons (7.25 tonnes)

DATE BUILT: unknown

RIG: Lateen

CREW: 3

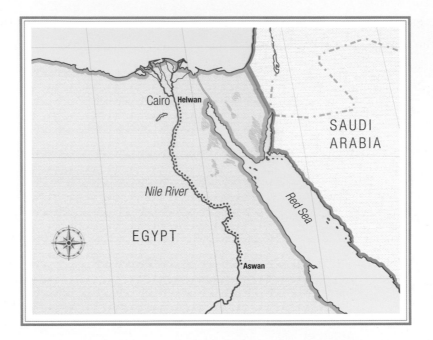

A Nile Adventure
Arabia

★ ★ ★

AS DAWN SWEPT AWAY the last vestiges of night, Willard Price looked down over the side of the boat on the townscape drifting past below him. The shape of roofs, narrow streets, and open courtyards, all picked out in the brilliance of the rapidly rising sun. But there were no people to be seen, for this townscape was buried underwater, submerged by the lake created by the original Aswan Dam (now known as the Aswan Low Dam). Price was seeing at firsthand the clash between modernity and the ancient world, where the waters of the Nile were corralled to control the fertility of the land downstream, drowning the Nubian villages, the farmlands, and even the temple of Isis—whose 60ft (18.3m) tower was the only thing to break the surface and which has since been dismantled and relocated to protect its history.

Willard Price was a journalist, an author, and, allegedly, an American spy. In 1939, when he set out to travel down the Nile, he was 52 years old and a seasoned adventurer, but nonetheless this trip held some potential dangers. Not the least of these was his choice of transport: a 20ft (6.1m) felucca called Arabia, crewed by two Nubians. The boat that was to be his home for 74 days and 600 miles (1,100km) was equipped with two oars and a lateen sail. The stern was covered by an awning under which Price slept; forward was a tiny fo'c'sle into which the Nubians squeezed at night, and amidships was the galley. Price had been offered the use of a dahabeah, a barge-like vessel twice as long as the felucca and for only half the cost, but he wanted to see ancient Egypt, the Egypt that seemed to be disappearing in the sweep of modern civilization, and the tiny felucca suited his purposes well.

And Price did see ancient Egypt. He visited the island of Bahrif, the quarries at Silsila, and the farms bordering the Nile—scenes from Egyptian tomb reliefs coming to life all around him. The oasis city of Helwan was the last stop before Cairo. Then, as Price and his crew set out on the final leg, a huge sandstorm swept in from the south. The tiny felucca corkscrewed down the river until, flung onto its side by the force of the gale, it deposited the men and their supplies into the churning water. After three hours struggling unsuccessfully to right the little felucca, they saw three fishing boats appearing from out of the gloom. The men were hauled aboard, the felucca was raised, and Price traveled the last five miles to Cairo in a borrowed djellaba and a taxi.

Avenger

*U*FFA *F*OX *DEFIED THE ACCEPTED LAWS OF PHYSICS WHEN HE DESIGNED A DINGHY THAT CLIMBED HER BOW WAVE AND PLANED OVER THE WATER, THEREBY DOUBLING HER SPEED AT ONE STROKE. A*ND THEN HE HAD THE AUDACITY TO SAIL HER ACROSS THE* C*HANNEL AND THRASH THE* F*RENCH TOO...*

JOURNEY: Cowes, UK, to Le Havre, France, and back
BOAT NAME: *Avenger*
CAPTAIN: Uffa Fox
DATE: 1928
DISTANCE: 200 nautical miles (370km)

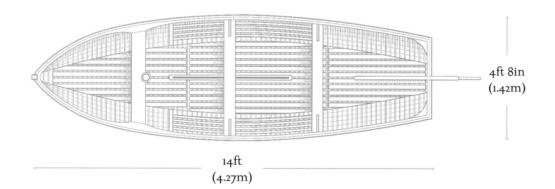

4ft 8in
(1.42m)

14ft
(4.27m)

LENGTH: 14ft (4.27m)
BEAM: 4ft 8in (1.42m)
DRAFT: 8in (20cm)/5ft (1.52m)
(centerboard down)

DISPLACEMENT: 800lb (363kg)
DATE BUILT: 1928
RIG: Bermudan sloop
CREW: 3

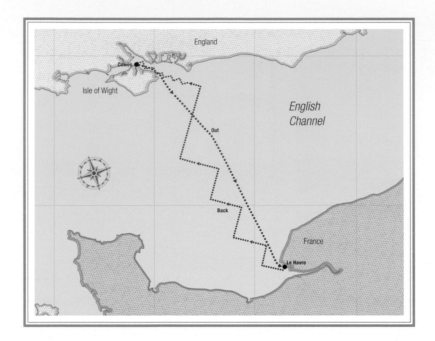

A Revolution at Sea
Avenger

★ ★ ★

BY 1928, THE ISLE OF WIGHT boatbuilder/designer Uffa Fox was living with his wife Alma on the River Medina on an old chain ferry he had converted into a workshop-cum-home. There was no running water, gas, or electricity on board, and the couple often had to live off the rabbits and fish Uffa caught and the berries Alma picked. That year, Uffa launched a 14ft

(4.27m) dinghy built to the International 14 class rule. The class was dominated by such established designers as Morgan Giles and Tom Thornycroft, who regarded the loud-mouthed Uffa as a pesky intruder into the genteel world of yacht racing. Uffa knew that if he was going to beat them, he would have to do something completely different.

Which is exactly what he proceeded to do. Ever since he had served his apprenticeship building hydroplanes and seaplanes at the yard of S.E. Saunders, he had had a feeling that the same principles could be applied to sailing boats—if only the front ends were a little finer and the back ends were a little flatter. His *Avenger* was the first boat to embody this principle fully. By lifting herself onto her bow wave and "planing" over the water, she defied the laws of physics that said a boat could only travel at its so-called "hull speed"—about 1.34 times the square root of its own waterline length. The results were dramatic. At that year's Prince of Wales Cup, *Avenger* finished more than five minutes ahead of her nearest rival and lapped 14 other boats.

After winning 20 races, Uffa decided to test his boat overseas. He and two friends loaded *Avenger* with all the equipment they would need and sailed her across the Channel to Le Havre—a journey most yachtsmen would undertake with trepidation in an open boat—to take part in the annual town regatta. After winning three races in two days, they tacked their way back across the Channel, arriving home a week later, just in time for breakfast. *Avenger* would continue her extraordinary success, winning 52 firsts, two seconds and three thirds out of 57 starts. Uffa had achieved nothing less than a revolution in yacht design, which would have a profound effect on every racing dinghy that followed. Despite his often belligerent attitude, he would go on to become one of the most successful designers of his generation—not least for his invention of the airborne lifeboats credited with saving hundreds of lives during World War II.

Gypsy Moth IV

She was designed and built by the top British yacht-building team and took Francis Chichester safely around the world, breaking several sailing records along the way. So why did the great man hate Gipsy Moth IV so much?

ROUTE: Plymouth to Plymouth, UK, via the world
BOAT NAME: *Gypsy Moth IV*
CAPTAIN: Francis Chichester
DATE: 1966–67
DISTANCE: 28,500 nautical miles (52,780km)

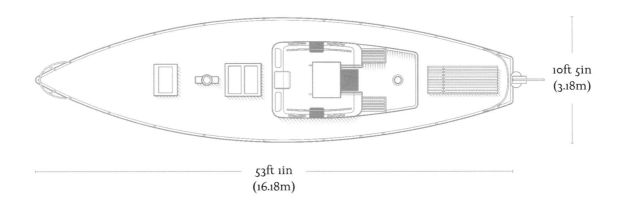

10ft 5in
(3.18m)

53ft 1in
(16.18m)

LENGTH: 53ft 1in (16.18m)
BEAM: 10ft 5in (3.18m)
DRAFT: 7ft 9in (2.36m)
DISPLACEMENT: 11.5 tons (10.43 tonnes)

DATE BUILT: 1966
RIG: Ketch
CREW: 1

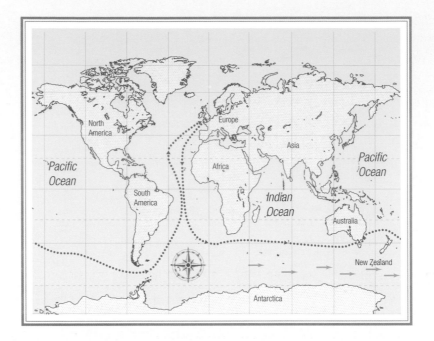

The Boat Chichester Loved to Hate
Gypsy Moth IV

★ ★ ★

SAILORS ARE A SUPERSTITIOUS LOT, and Francis Chichester was no exception. When his wife failed to smash the bottle against the bow of his new yacht at her launching ceremony in March 1966, he was immediately thrown into panic: "I was horrified," he later wrote, "my heart sank; I thought, what a terrible omen." Worse was to come during sea trials the following day when *Gipsy Moth IV* heeled over, "so that the masts were horizontal, parallel with the water surface." Despite the addition of 2,400lb (1,090kg) of lead, the yacht remained tender and hard to handle, and the early chapters of Chichester's book about his subsequent voyage are a long litany of the problems and shortcomings of his most detested yacht. To add insult to injury, she had cost 50 percent more to build than had been expected, and much of Chichester's time in the months before his departure was spent in the raising of the money to pay for her.

Despite this inauspicious start, Chichester made a fast passage to Australia and would have achieved his mission, to beat the tea-clippers' 100-day benchmark, if his self-steering hadn't packed up 2,300 miles (4,260km) from Sydney. Instead, he wasted valuable time trying to fix it and arrived in Australia exhausted and emaciated after 107 days at sea. The second part of his circumnavigation wasn't much better, as he suffered a 140-degree capsize before he even reached Cape Horn. By the time he got back to Plymouth, after 226 days at sea, he wanted to have nothing more to do with the boat that had taken him around the world, and immediately donated her to the National Maritime Museum. "*Gipsy Moth IV* has no sentimental value for me at all," he wrote. "She is cantankerous and difficult and needs a crew of three—a man to navigate, an elephant to move the tiller and a 3ft 6in chimpanzee with arms 8ft long to get about below and work some of the gear."

But regardless of this personal antagonism, Chichester and *Gipsy Moth IV* did set several records, including that for the longest and fastest single-handed voyage in a small boat. His achievements were headline news—helped by recent developments in radio technology that meant he was able to feed updates to the media at regular intervals—and inspired a generation of sailors to take up single-handed racing. The stage was set for the famous Golden Globe and other single-handed races that were to follow.

Cormorant

For Christian Beamish, sailing 600 miles (1,100km) down the west coast of Mexico in a 19ft (5.8m) open boat was a spiritual mission: he wanted to immerse himself in nature and reconnect with his ancestral dna. He ended up getting more than he bargained for.

ROUTE: San Diego, California, to Isla Cedros, Mexico

BOAT NAME: *Cormorant*

CAPTAIN: Christian Beamish

DATE: 2009

DISTANCE: 400 nautical miles (740km)

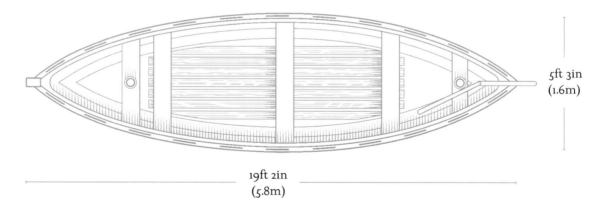

5ft 3in (1.6m)

19ft 2in (5.8m)

LENGTH: 19ft 2in (5.8m)

BEAM: 5ft 3in (1.6m)

DRAFT: 8in (20cm)

DISPLACEMENT: 275lb (125kg)

DATE BUILT: 2005-07

RIG: Yawl

CREW: 1

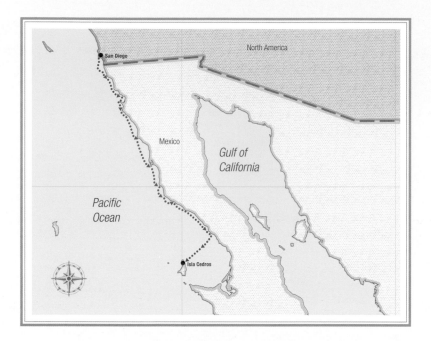

Ocean Therapy
Cormorant

★ ★ ★

IT WAS A VERY 21ST-CENTURY VOYAGE. Christian Beamish, a surfer, surfboard shaper, and writer, was an associate editor on *The Surfer's Journal* suffering an existential crisis: he was lovelorn, drinking far too much, and popping Prozac to get rid of his lingering malaise. He longed to escape the materialistic, over-technological world of urban California and connect with his "blood memory," the elemental ancestral experience that he felt was buried deep in his DNA. Experienced in making his own surfboards in the past and even the tools for the craft, Beamish turned his hand to building himself a boat: the 19ft (5.8m) long *Cormorant*, a Ness Yawl based on the traditional fishing boats of the Shetland Isles in Scotland—albeit adapted for DIY construction in plywood and epoxy.

After a few experimental cruises, Beamish quit his job and set off on his adventure: 600 miles (1,100km) from San Diego to Bahía Magdalena in Mexico. His plan was to live on the boat, be at one with nature, and ride some waves along the way, and to this end he packed his little boat with food, equipment—and two surfboards. Over the following two months, he went through everything you'd expect to go through sailing in a small boat along such an exposed coast: he had lots of wind, he had no wind, he had to row a lot, he got stuck in algae, his boat was smashed up in a storm, and he was visited by a swarm of bees (actually, one of the more bizarre episodes!). It's hardly *Moby Dick*, but along the way he does have a genuine adventure, due at least in part to his very lack of experience—he repeatedly has to be rescued and hosted by local fishermen and their families. The fact he eventually gives up and puts his boat on a ship home 200 miles (370km) short of his intended destination only emphasizes the scale of his ambition: he has taken on more than he is capable of and is lucky not to have been drowned. Next time, he'll know more and go farther.

By the end of the voyage, he's helmed his boat for hours on end across stormy waters, he's sailed alone across a moonlit sea, he's been woken up at night by the breath of passing whales, he's caught, cooked, and eaten his own fish, and he's befriended a whole host of interesting characters. He's discovered the elemental ancestral experience, weaned himself off Prozac, and got the material for his first book, *The Voyage of the Comorant*, released in 2012. A great result by any reckoning.

Egret

The New Haven sharpie was conceived as a simple, cheap working boat to fish for oysters along America's east coast. Ralph Munroe (aka "the Commodore") pioneered it as a seagoing yachts, using local knowledge to perform hair-raising "sharpie tricks"—including sailing across a shallow sandbar at night in a raging gale.

JOURNEY: Coconut Grove to Lake Worth, Florida
BOAT NAME: *Egret*
CAPTAIN: Ralph M. Munroe
DATE: *ca.*1887
DISTANCE: 74 nautical miles (137km)

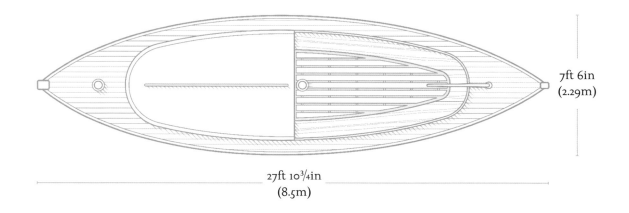

7ft 6in
(2.29m)

27ft 10³/₄in
(8.5m)

LENGTH: 27ft 10³/₄in (8.5m)
BEAM: 7ft 6in (2.29m)
DRAFT: 10in (25cm)
DISPLACEMENT: 5,000lb (2,268kg)

DATE BUILT: 1886
RIG: Gaff ketch
CREW: 2

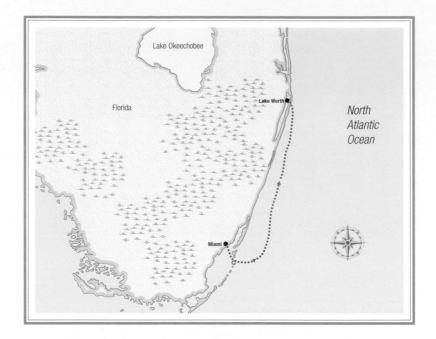

The Commodore's Story
Egret

★ ★ ★

RALPH MUNROE'S SHARPIE BOAT made a strange sight when she was unloaded from the steamer's deck in Key West, Florida in 1881. With her boxy sides and shallow keel, she was very different from the indigenous workboats, and the general opinion was that she would be useless except for going downwind. Munroe soon proved the locals wrong and, over the following years, pioneered the type not only for sailing on the lakes but for offshore sailing too. His 28ft (8.5m) *Egret*, in particular, has been described as the most seaworthy sharpie ever built—although the boat's towering reputation must be at least partly due to Munroe's skill in handling her and the vivid descriptions of these exploits in his autobiography, *The Commodore's Story*, published in 1930.

One incident from the book perfectly illustrates the boat's abilities. Munroe and a crew were sailing from Coconut Grove, Miami, to Lake Worth, on the east coast of Florida, when they were caught in a gale. The two other boats out on the water simply turned around and headed back to Cape Florida but, although night was falling and the storm showed no sign of abating, Munroe decided to simply tuck in "a reef or two" and carry on. "Harder and harder it came down on us," he writes, "but the little boat never whimpered. The sea? Well, just the [Gulf] Stream in a northeaster, as any skipper can describe it—capping, and phosphorescent in the darkness, with little foot to it." Eventually, they spotted the glimmer of Jupiter lighthouse and the breakers at the entrance of Lake Worth (as it was then). With the mainsail lowered and centerboard raised, they negotiated the channel (now known as Palm Beach Inlet) and "with one wild rush we were through the breakers and foam, over the bar, and inside the point of beach"—to the consternation of a lone fisherman moored up quietly on the other side of the shallow bar.

Tales such as this not only cemented the sharpie's reputation in the mind of the sailing public but also promoted Munroe's career as a yacht designer. The following day, he took a party of locals sailing on Lake Worth and, as a strong northerly sent other boats scurrying back to their moorings, he performed his "sharpie tricks," swooping down the lake "like an arrow from the bow" and "ending the performance with a sensational jibe and round-up." The "performance" duly earned him a commission for another boat.

Seraffyn

She's the boat that launched 50,000 dreams, as aspiring sailors the world over tried to emulate the free-roaming lifestyle of her original builders. Yet the origins of Seraffyn's design were deeply unfashionable when she was conceived during the postwar boom.

JOURNEY: Newport Beach to Newport Beach, California, via the world
BOAT NAME: *Seraffyn*
CAPTAIN: Larry Pardey
DATE: 1968–79
DISTANCE: 45,000 nautical miles (83,340km)

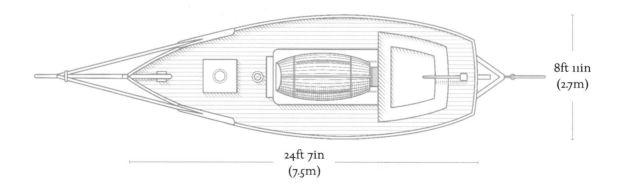

8ft 11in
(2.7m)

24ft 7in
(7.5m)

LENGTH: 24ft 7in (7.5m)
BEAM: 8ft 11in (2.7m)
DRAFT: 4ft 8in (1.4m)
DISPLACEMENT: 5.2 tons (4.8 tonnes)

DATE BUILT: 1964–8
RIG: Cutter
CREW: 2

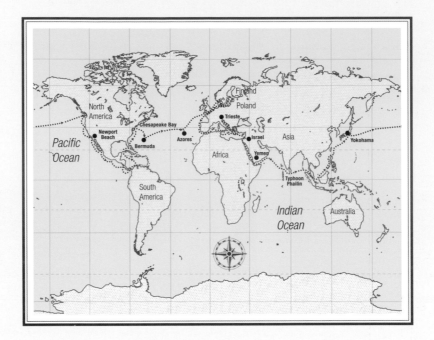

Small is Beautiful
Seraffyn

★ ★ ★

LYLE HESS WAS SWIMMING AGAINST the tide when he designed the 25ft (7.6m) wooden cutter *Renegade* in 1950. Traditional working boats were firmly out of fashion, and within a few years wood had been completely eclipsed by fiberglass as the building material of choice. Yet Hess's jaunty design, based on the lines of an Itchen ferry from the Solent, UK, captured the timeless spirit of these old boats while looking utterly capable and contemporary. *Renegade* caught the eye of a young Canadian boat nut called Larry Pardey who asked Hess to make a few modifications—including replacing the archaic gaff rig with a Bermudan—and started building his own dream boat behind a printing plant in Costa Mesa, California. Larry was soon joined by his girlfriend Lin, and the couple were duly married in October 1968, three weeks before their first "baby," the 24ft 7in (7.5m) cutter *Seraffyn*, was launched.

It was the start of a legend. For the next 11 years, Lin and Larry sailed the engineless boat 45,000 miles (83,340km) around the world, visiting Mexico, the Caribbean, Europe, the Baltic, the Mediterranean, the Red Sea, Southeast Asia, Japan, and Canada. With just $5,000 in the bank at the start of the voyage, they supported themselves by writing articles for magazines (mainly Lin) and working on other people's boats (mainly Larry). Their best calling card was *Seraffyn* herself, which they maintained to an enviously high standard—even her bilges were varnished throughout and clean enough to eat your lunch off. Sailing without an engine was a relative rarity and sealed their reputations as virtuoso sailors—most modern sailors would balk at going into harbor under sail alone, never mind sailing around the world. Their first book, *Cruising in Seraffyn*, was published in 1976, to be followed by a string of books describing their adventures and offering practical advice for fellow sailors.

By the time they made it back to Newport Beach, California, in November 1979, they had developed a cult following and *Seraffyn* was snapped up by a buyer for nearly twice her asking price. The 29ft (8.8m) *Taleisin* followed, also designed by Lyle Hess, on which they sailed another 80,000 miles (15,000km), including a further one and a half circumnavigations. Meanwhile, the rest of the sailing world was catching up and a whole fleet of little *Seraffyns* and *Taleisins* began to spring up around the world. Some were even built in fiberglass. For the Pardeys, it was due vindication of their motto: "Go simple, go small, go now."

Tilikum

Two men, a dugout canoe, and 40,000 miles (74,000km) of ocean: it sounds like a recipe for disaster. Captain Voss's epic not-quite-round-the-world voyage brought him fame and fortune but exposed him to accusations of bullying and even murder.

ROUTE: Victoria, Canada, to London, UK, via Sydney, Australia
BOAT NAME: *Tilikum*
CAPTAIN: John Voss
DATE: 1901–04
DISTANCE: 40,000 nautical miles (74,000km)

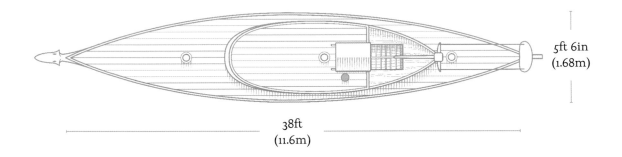

5ft 6in
(1.68m)

38ft
(11.6m)

LENGTH: 38ft (11.6m)
BEAM: 5ft 6in (1.68m)
DRAFT: 1ft 6in (0.45m)
DISPLACEMENT: Unknown

DATE BUILT: *ca*.1850
RIG: Schooner
CREW: 2

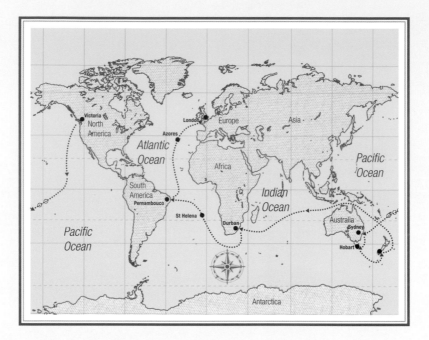

The Troublesome Voyage of Captain Voss
Tilikum

★ ★ ★

A CHANCE ENCOUNTER LED TO ONE of sailing's most extraordinary ocean voyages. In a bar in Victoria, BC, in the spring of 1901 Captain John Voss met journalist Norman Luxton and got talking about Joshua Slocum's epic circumnavigation on his boat *Spray*. Slocum had published a book about his adventures, which had become a bestseller, and Luxton was keen to emulate his success. But how could they improve on Slocum's record? Simple, said Voss: do the trip on a smaller boat. And the boat he came up with was truly original: a 38ft (11.6m) long dugout canoe, carved from a single, massive cedar tree that was 50 years old when Voss bought it from a native woman for C$80. Voss raised the boat's topsides by 7 inches (18cm), strengthened the hull with oak frames, built a 5ft (1.5m) by 8ft (2.4m) cabin and fitted a three-masted schooner rig. He named the boat *Tilikum*, meaning "friend" in Chinook.

In fact, the journey was anything but friendly. Setting off from Victoria in May 1901, they sailed for five months across the Pacific, covering 10,000 miles (18,500 km), quarreling the whole way. After hitting a reef off Suva, Fiji, and being left for dead by Voss, Luxton finally had enough and took a steamer to Sydney. He wrote: "Dangerous as were the storms and calms of the Pacific, they were as nothing compared to the clash of our personalities. Before we ever reached Apia, Samoa, we hated each other, and I was certain Voss intended to do me harm."

Voss's next mate fared even worse. During a storm en route to Australia, the young Walter Bergent fell over the side (along with the compass) and drowned although in private Luxton suggested Voss probably killed him in a drunken fury. Whatever the truth, Voss navigated 1,200 miles (2,200 km) to Sydney without the compass, in itself a remarkable feat of seamanship.

Several changes of mate later, in September 1904 Voss finally made it to London, three years and three months after leaving Canada, having traveled some 40,000 miles (74,000 km). Like other globetrotting adventurers, he lectured widely about his voyage and in 1913 published his sailing memoirs as *The Venturesome Voyages of Captain Voss*. Luxton's own version was published posthumously in 1971 by his daughter. As for *Tilikum*, she went through a succession of owners in the UK, before being repatriated to Canada in 1930. She was restored and exhibited at the Maritime Museum of British Columbia, where she can still be seen today.

Joshua

The steel ketch Joshua is famous for not winning the Golden Globe Race in 1968, because her skipper Bernard Moitessier couldn't face returning to the "snake pit" and sailed on to Tahiti instead. But the Frenchman wasn't quite as crazy as he might have seemed...

JOURNEY: Plymouth, UK, to Tahiti
BOAT NAME: *Joshua*
CAPTAIN: Bernard Moitessier
DATE: 1968–69
DISTANCE: 37,455 nautical miles (69,370km)

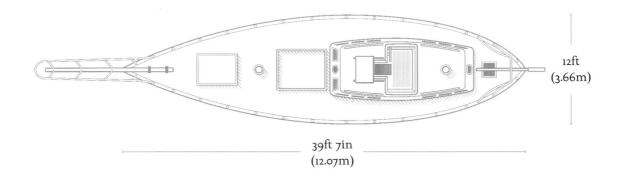

12ft
(3.66m)

39ft 7in
(12.07m)

LENGTH: 39ft 7in (12.07m)
BEAM: 12ft (3.66m)
DRAFT: 5ft 3in (1.6m)
DISPLACEMENT: 14.3 tons (13 tonnes)

DATE BUILT: 1962
RIG: Ketch
CREW: 1

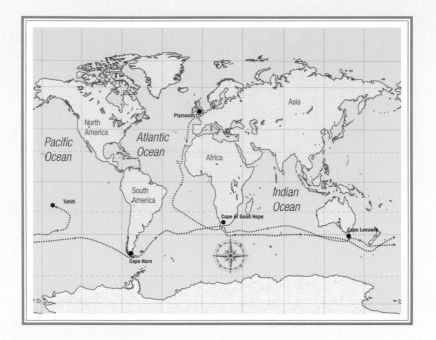

Fast and Free
Joshua

★ ★ ★

IT'S ONE OF THE MOST FAMOUS STORIES in sailing history: the lone Frenchman sailing in the very first around-the-world race who, rather than head north to almost certain victory, decides to abandon the race and carry on sailing halfway around the world to "save his soul." How very romantic; how very French! But while Moitessier is often portrayed as a sailing eccentric, what's often overlooked is that he was a wily sailor who achieved his superior speed through a radical sailing strategy that was quite contrary to the prevailing practices at the time.

After an eventful upbringing in Asia, Moitessier set off on a series of sailing adventures in the 1950s, first in Asia then across the Atlantic to the Caribbean, where he was eventually shipwrecked. The book he wrote about his experiences, *Vagabond des Mers du Sud*, was an immediate success and allowed him to build a new boat: a steel ketch he named *Joshua* after his hero Joshua Slocum. In 1963 he set off with his wife Françoise for a honeymoon cruise to the Caribbean, through the Panama Canal, then on to the Galapagos Islands and French Polynesia. But rather than sail home via the Suez Canal, they doubled back on themselves and headed east, down around Cape Horn and back up the Atlantic. When they arrived in France 126 days later, they had set a record for the longest-ever nonstop voyage by a yacht.

It was on this journey that Moitessier made a startling discovery. Whereas conventional wisdom advised reducing sail and towing drogues to slow a boat down in heavy weather, he discovered the opposite approach worked best on *Joshua*. By allowing her to sail fast and free, he could keep ahead of breaking waves and sail more safely. It was a hair-raising and exhausting practice, but it also made for fast passages. When the time came for the Golden Globe Challenge two years later, Moitessier not only had a well-tested boat, he also had a sailing strategy that put him ahead of his rivals. So while Robin Knox-Johnston was deliberately slowing his boat down in the Southern Ocean, Moitessier was surfing down the waves with aplomb, and steadily gaining on the Englishman. If he hadn't had a penchant for philosophy, Moitessier might well have won the race and earned himself a place in the record books. Instead, he turned his voyage into a 37,455-mile (69,370km) meditation and wrote a bestselling book about the experience. So who really won the race?

Said

Retired ship's mechanic Evgeny Gvozdev wasn't going to let a shortage of cash stop him from achieving his dream. He built a 11ft 10in (3.6m) microcruiser on his balcony and sailed it around the world—equaling a world record (or very nearly).

JOURNEY: Makhachkala, Russia, to Makhachkala, Russia
BOAT NAME: *Said*
CAPTAIN: Evgeny Gvozdev
DATE: 1999–2003
DISTANCE: 30–40,000 nautical miles (55,600–74,000km)

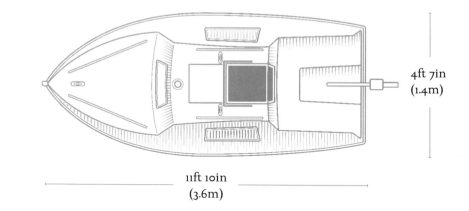

4ft 7in
(1.4m)

11ft 10in
(3.6m)

LENGTH: 11ft 10in (3.6m)
BEAM: 4ft 7in (1.4m)
DRAFT: 2ft 8 in (0.8m)
WEIGHT: 770lb (350kg)

DATE BUILT: 1998–99
RIG: Sloop
CREW: 1

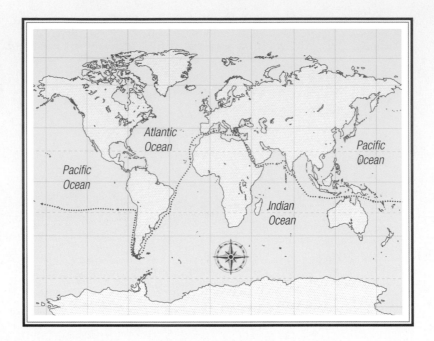

Third Time Unlucky
Said

★ ★ ★

After the collapse of the Soviet Union in 1991, Evgeny Gvozdev wasted no time in celebrating his newfound freedom by sailing around the world on an 18ft (5.5m) yacht called *Lena* in 1992–96. Despite being attacked and robbed of most of his possessions by Somalian pirates, he lived to tell the tale and for some time *Lena* was exhibited in a Russian museum. By 1999, he had retired and decided it was time for another sailing adventure—only this time he would build the yacht himself. The 11ft 10in (3.6m) long *Said* was built, hanging from the balcony of his first-floor apartment, using scraps of timber and other materials he found on the streets of Makhachkala on the shore of the Caspian Sea. Once finished, the boat was lowered into the back of a truck and driven to the sea—first the Caspian and then, for the main voyage, the Black Sea. (He was offered a fully equipped yacht in Canada for free, but refused on the grounds that his voyage must start and finish in Russia and be made on a Russian-built boat.)

When Gvozdev set off on his madcap journey July 2, 1999, he had no engine, no GPS, no autopilot, no satellite phone, no VHF radio, no water distiller, and no solar battery—all the things most long-distance sailors take for granted. He navigated using a plastic sextant, a compass, and charts that he swapped with other sailors along the way. He could hardly move inside the cabin of his tiny boat, so crammed was it with food and water—and not without reason. One particularly grueling passage involved 90 days at sea, of which 20 were becalmed. His average speed was 2 knots (3.7km/h)—slower than walking pace.

It was a remarkable journey by any standards, and put him on a par with the Australian sailor Serge Testa, who holds the official record for sailing the smallest boat single-handedly around the world, a journey he made in the 11ft 10in (3.6m) *Acrohc Australis* in 1983–87. *Said* is variously described as 3.6m or 3.7m—10cm (or 4in) that make the difference between equaling the record or not. Not content with that, in October 2008 Gvozdev set off again, this time on an 18ft (5.5m) yacht identical to *Lena*, intent on attempting a third circumnavigation. Three months later, his body was found washed up on a beach near Rome, close to his stranded yacht, with a large gash to his head. Gvozdev's luck had finally run out. With so many boats racing around the world in ever-shorter times (the current record stands at 45 days), it's easy to forget just what an achievement this is. Evgeny Gvozdev serves to remind us.

Liberia III

A fascination with what happened to the minds and bodies of shipwrecked sailors drove a young German doctor to cross the Atlantic in a canvas kayak to "test the durability of the human machine." His conclusion? It's all in the mind.

JOURNEY: Las Palmas, Canary Islands, to St Martin
BOAT NAME: *Liberia III*
CAPTAIN: Hannes Lindemann
DATE: 1956
DISTANCE: 3,400 nautical miles (6,300km)

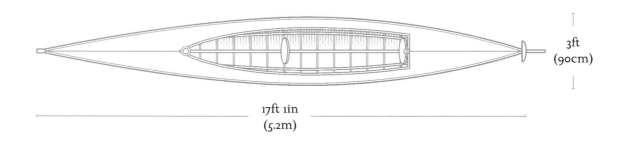

3ft
(90cm)

17ft 1in
(5.2m)

LENGTH: 17ft 1in (5.2m)
BEAM: 3ft (0.9m)
DRAFT: 2in (5cm) (unloaded)
DISPLACEMENT: 59lb (27kg)

DATE BUILT: 1956
RIG: Gunter-rigged ketch
CREW: 1

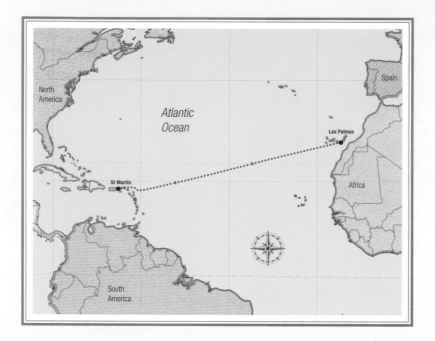

A Journey of the Mind
Liberia III

★ ★ ★

WHAT HAPPENS TO THE MIND when someone has to fend for themselves alone at sea for weeks on end? How can shipwrecked sailors cope both physically and mentally with extreme hardship and limited supplies of food and drink? And should a castaway ever drink saltwater? These were the questions Hannes Lindemann pondered while working for the

Firestone Rubber Company in Liberia. The young German doctor first put his ideas to the test by crossing the Atlantic from Las Palmas to Haiti in a heavily adapted dugout canoe in October–December 1955. It was while he was recuperating from that voyage that he discovered his real mission. "Through voodoo," he later wrote, "I learned that one can, by deep concentration, a kind of self-hypnosis, change one's fundamental attitude toward a problem, that, ultimately, through voodoo, one can rid oneself of fears and doubts."

Less than a year later, he was at it again, this time with a lightweight folding kayak with two square sails added for downwind passages. Sailing 3,400 miles (6,300km) on such a frail craft would allow him to experience the feelings of the "lonely castaway," he wrote. "By suffering the utmost from the elements, I could test the durability of the human machine, and in a cockleshell like mine I would learn much that we need to know about survival at sea." And the technique he would use to overcome his difficulties was mind control. Using the system of autogenic training advocated by J.H. Schultz, he fortified his mind through prayer and meditation and through repeating mantras such as "I will make it" and "Keep going west."

In October 1956, Lindemann set off again from Las Palmas in his canvas kayak, and was soon able to try out his new theory. After four weeks at sea, he started hearing voices. After eight weeks he was chatting merrily with an African boy who turned out to be the boat's rubber outrigger. Then in mid-December, the canoe capsized not once but twice, and he had to cling to the hull for dear life, as he drifted in and out of consciousness chanting, "Keep going west. Never give up." Finally, after 72 days at sea, he landed at St Martin in the Caribbean. He had lost 25 percent of his bodyweight and his heart rate was dangerously low, but he had proven his thesis. "I know now that the mind succumbs before the body, that although lack of sleep, thirst or hunger weaken the body, it is the undisciplined mind that drives the castaway to panic and heedless action. [. . .] Morale is the single most important factor in survival."

Kathena Nui

More people have walked on the moon than have sailed around the world single-handed and nonstop the "wrong" way (i.e. east to west). Yet, aged 60, that's exactly what Wilfried Erdmann decided to do. If only he'd remembered to pack enough food.

JOURNEY: Cuxhaven to Cuxhaven, Germany, via the world
BOAT NAME: *Kathena Nui*
CAPTAIN: Wilfried Erdmann
DATE: 2000–1
DISTANCE: 32,000 nautical miles (59,260km)

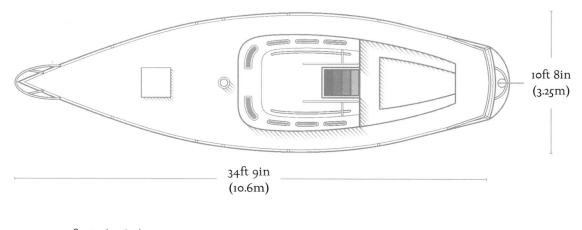

10ft 8in
(3.25m)

34ft 9in
(10.6m)

LENGTH: 34ft 9in (10.6m)
BEAM: 10ft 8in (3.25m)
DRAFT: 5ft 7in (1.7m)
DISPLACEMENT: 5.9 tons (5.4 tonnes)

DATE BUILT: 1984
RIG: Bermudan sloop
CREW: 1

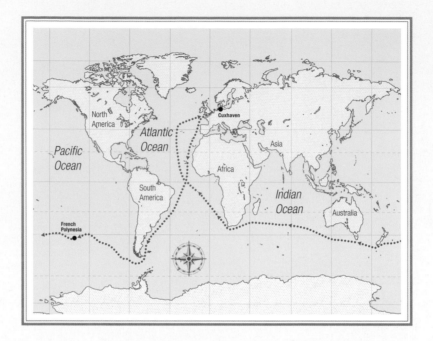

Fish, Fish Everywhere...
Kathena Nui

★ ★ ★

MAY 28, 1967 WILL ALWAYS BE REMEMBERED by sailors as the day Sir Francis Chichester returned to Plymouth after 226 days at sea and set a record for the fastest single-handed circumnavigation of the world. A few weeks earlier, on March 13, Wilfried Erdmann set off from Gibraltar on a 25ft (7.6m) wooden boat on his first circumnavigation, and must have passed Chichester as he sailed down the Atlantic. So unpublicized was his trip, however, that when he returned to Germany 421 days later, no one believed he had sailed around the world. Eventually, after offering proof that he had done what he claimed, he was accepted as the first German sailor to have completed a single-handed circumnavigation of the globe.

But that wasn't enough for Erdmann. After a 1,011-day honeymoon cruise around the world with his wife Astrid in 1969–72, he decided to embark on the ultimate sailing challenge: to travel around the world single-handed and nonstop (like Robin Knox-Johnston in '69). This time he had a boat purpose-built for the journey: the 35ft (10.6m) *Kathena Nui*, which he packed to the gunwales with food and other supplies. In June 1985, he completed his third loop in a relatively speedy 271 days, becoming the first German to do it single-handed and nonstop.

And that should have been that. Except that, even aged 60, Erdmann hadn't quite finished with the sea. There was one last challenge he wanted to take on: sailing around the world single-handed and nonstop the "wrong way," i.e. from east to west, against the prevailing winds and currents (like Chay Blyth in '71). And so, on August 14, 2000, Erdmann set off from Cuxhaven once again. Everything went swimmingly as he headed down the Atlantic, but as he rounded Cape Horn and faced the full brunt of the Southern Ocean, he realized why it was called going the "wrong way." Faced with relentless gales, at times he found himself actually going backward. To make matters worse, he broke one of his ribs and had to crawl around the boat on his hands and knees. But his main worry was running out of food. He had stocked up for 310 days, but the bad weather meant he would almost certainly take longer. Moreover, he couldn't supplement his diet with fish as, curiously, he was allergic to them. When he eventually arrived back in Cuxhaven on July 23, 2001, after 343 days at sea, he had lost 22lb (10kg) in weight. And this time no one doubted his achievement.

Crusoe's periagua

POOR OLD ROBINSON CRUSOE. STUCK ON A DESERTED ISLAND FOR YEARS AND WHEN HE DOES FINALLY BUILD HIMSELF A BOAT HE IS ALMOST SWEPT OUT TO SEA. IT'S ALL PART OF THE MORAL EDUCATION HE HAS TO UNDERGO BEFORE HE'S ALLOWED TO LEAVE THE ISLAND.

JOURNEY: From the south to the north side of the island
BOAT NAME: Unnamed
CAPTAIN: Robinson Crusoe
DATE: 1663
DISTANCE: 10 nautical miles (18km)

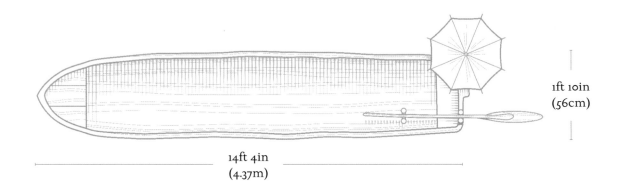

1ft 10in
(56cm)

14ft 4in
(4.37m)

LENGTH: 14ft 4in (4.37m)
BEAM: 1ft 10in (56cm)
DRAFT: 7in (18cm)
DISPLACEMENT: 300 lb (136kg)

DATE BUILT: 1661–3
RIG: Bermudan
CREW: 1

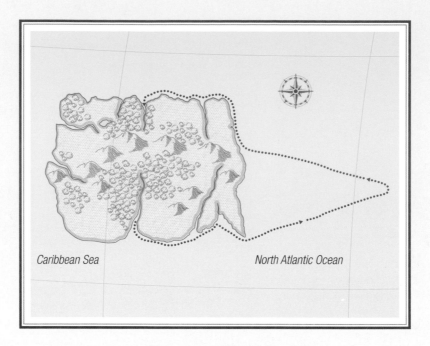

Caribbean Sea

North Atlantic Ocean

Castaway Cruise
Crusoe's periagua

★ ★ ★

AFTER NEARLY FOUR YEARS LIVING as a castaway, Robinson Crusoe has got things quite well sorted: he has a large, comfortable cave as his main dwelling and a summer house on the other side of the island for holidays; he's learned how to harvest barley and rice and how to make tools, baskets, and pottery; he has a pet parrot and a pet goat; and he's even figured out how to make bread. In sum, he is as content now as he has ever been. But despite this, the urge to travel farther afield and explore other islands in the archipelago is strong. So he starts to build a boat.

His first attempt is a massive canoe cut from a cedar trunk 5ft 10in (1.8m) in diameter at its base and more than 22ft (6.7m) long. Crusoe spends five months "hacking and hewing" at the wood to make a beautiful *periagua* "big enough to have carried six-and-twenty men." Only when it's finished does he realize he has no way of getting it to the sea. He contemplates digging a canal, but works out it would take him 12 years to do that. The moral of the story? "Now I saw, though too late, the folly of beginning a work before we count the cost, and before we judge rightly of our own strength to go through with it."

It takes nearly two years for Crusoe to build his next (much smaller) canoe and cut a canal half a mile long to float it from the building site to the sea. He then fits a mast and sail, erects an umbrella in the stern, and, stocked up with two dozen loaves of barley bread, a pot of rice, half a goat, and a small bottle of rum, sets off to "view the circumference of [his] little kingdom." The trip is not a success. Despite waiting three days for the right conditions, Crusoe is swept out to sea by a strong current and is unable to paddle back to shore. There's a moral here too: "Now I looked back upon my desolate, solitary island, as the most pleasant place in the world; and all the happiness my heart could wish for was to be there again. [. . .] Thus we never see the true state of our condition, till it is illustrated to us by its contraries; nor know how to value what we enjoy, but by the want of it."

Crusoe is saved only when a friendly breeze springs up that allows him to sail back to land. He moors the canoe in a nearby creek and, chastened, hurries off to his "country house." He's not tempted to set off on another boating adventure for several more years.

Chidiock Tichborne

A Drascombe Lugger is a fine boat for a family sail or some coastal hopping, but sailing across an ocean? Forget it. Or at least that's what everyone thought until Webb Chiles sailed Chidiock Tichborne most of the way around the world.

JOURNEY: San Diego, California to Las Palmas, Canary Islands, via the world
BOAT NAME: *Chidiock Tichborne*
CAPTAIN: Webb Chiles
DATE: 1978–84
DISTANCE: 20,000 nautical miles (37,000km)

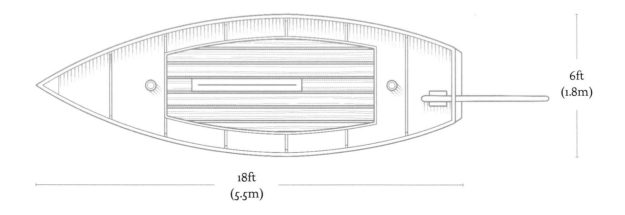

18ft
(5.5m)

6ft
(1.8m)

LENGTH: 18ft (5.5m)
BEAM: 6ft (1.8m)
DRAFT: 10in (25cm)/4ft (1.2m) centerboard down

DISPLACEMENT: 900lb (408kg)
DATE BUILT: 1978
RIG: Yawl
CREW: 1

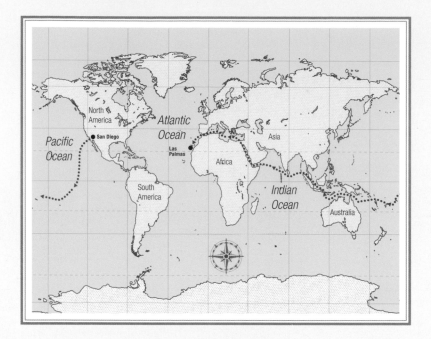

A Single Wave
Chidiock Tichborne

★ ★ ★

WEBB CHILES WAS HALFWAY BETWEEN Fiji and Vanuatu in the Pacific Ocean when he met his nemesis: a lone wave with his name on it. He had had a wild ride on his little boat *Chidiock Tichborne* since leaving Suva three days earlier, with 30-knot (56-kph) winds and 15ft (4.5m) waves pushing them both westward at a reckless pace. Finally, on May 10, 1980, the weather eased and he settled down for what he hoped would be his first good night's sleep of the voyage. It was not to be. Just before 10:30 p.m., he heard a clank and *Chidiock* pitchpoled as she slid down a wave, literally spinning stern over bow. "One moment I was sleeping wrapped in the tarp on the port side of the cockpit," he later wrote, "and the next I was flying through the air, catapulted like a pebble." He swam back to the boat and found her lying on her starboard side, her mast 30 degrees underwater.

Capsizing far from land is every sailor's nightmare, but it was particularly dangerous for Chiles as *Chidiock* was an 18ft (5.5m) open boat—little more than a dinghy—with no deck or cabin to keep the water out. It was the kind of boat normally used for family sailing or a little cautious coastal cruising. No one had ever attempted to sail around the world in such a small craft. But Chiles had defied the skeptics and sailed more than 6,000 miles (11,100km) from San Diego across the Pacific to Fiji—already the longest voyage ever made in an open boat. And now one wave threatened to bring the whole adventure to an end.

Chiles managed to get the boat upright, but water came in as fast as he could bail it out and he had to let her wallow in the sea, only kept afloat by her buoyancy tanks. He drifted for two weeks, drinking two sips of water per day, before eventually spotting land and making a dash for shore in his emergency inflatable dinghy. Had he missed Émaé, one of the Shepherd Islands, his next landfall would have been Australia, 1,400 miles (2,600km) away to the west. Incredibly, the sea's currents deposited *Chidiock* on a beach a few miles farther south on the same island. After refitting the boat, he resumed his voyage four months later, sailing via Southeast Asia and the Red Sea, and across the Mediterranean to the Canary Islands. There, a second capsize while the boat was on a mooring put an end to his ambition of a complete circumnavigation. But by then he had already sailed 20,000 miles (37,000km)—a remarkable record by any standard.

Dove/Return of Dove

When he was 16, Robin Lee Graham told his parents he wanted a boat to sail the Pacific. Most parents would have laughed, but Graham's parents bought him a boat and helped him sail around the world. Trouble was, this boat came with strings attached—lots of them.

JOURNEY: Los Angeles to Los Angeles, California, via the world
BOAT NAME: *Dove/Return of Dove*
CAPTAIN: Robin Lee Graham
DATE: 1965–70
DISTANCE: 30,600 nautical miles (56,670km)

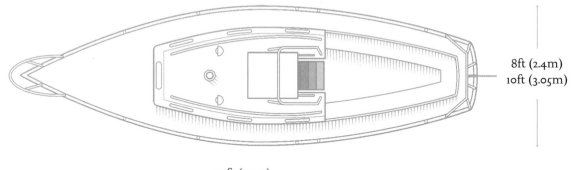

8ft (2.4m)
10ft (3.05m)

24ft (7.3m)
33ft (10.1m)

LENGTH: 24ft (7.3m)/33ft (10.1m)
BEAM: 8ft (2.4m)/10ft (3.05m)
DRAFT: 4ft (1.2m)/5ft (1.5m)
DISPLACEMENT: 4,350lb (1,980kg)/12,800lb

(5,800kg)
DATE BUILT: 1960/1968
RIG: Sloop/sloop
CREW: 1

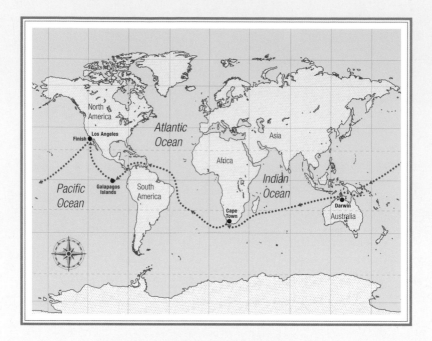

The Dove's Contract
Dove/Return of Dove

★ ★ ★

WHEN ROBIN LEE GRAHAM SAILED around the world single-handed in 1965–70, he had lots going for him. He had a relatively new boat, plenty of sailing experience for someone his age, the support of his parents, and the benefits of a major sponsor, *National Geographic* magazine. When he lost his mast in the Indian Ocean and had to sail 2,300 miles under jury rig to

Mauritius, a new mast was flown to him courtesy of *National Geographic* and Qantas. When his boat started falling apart in South Africa, he had her completely rebuilt and strengthened for the Atlantic crossing. And when he threatened to give up the voyage completely in South America, his sponsors bought him a new, bigger boat, complete with fully functioning auxiliary engine, two-way radio, and fridge. It was in many ways a privileged voyage.

But such privileges can also turn into a trap. When Graham fell in love with Patti Ratterree, five years his senior, in Fiji, he wanted to give everything up and start a life with her instead. But by then his father, who was also his agent, had signed various publishing deals, including a book and a series of articles in *National Geographic*, and wouldn't countenance his son dropping out. The rest of the circumnavigation turned into an emotional rollercoaster, as the boy-turned-man vacillated between the isolation of sailing alone and the euphoria of being reunited with Patti at various landfalls along the way. The couple were married in Darwin, Australia, only for Graham to leave again a few months later—he later confessed he seriously thought about scuttling the boat off South Africa rather than carry on with the voyage.

By the time Graham returned to Los Angeles in April 1970, he had sailed 30,600 miles (56,670km) and, at 21, was the youngest person to have sailed around the world single-handed. He was also a husband and almost a father—Patti gave birth to their daughter Quimby seven weeks later. His book about the voyage, *The Dove*, published in 1972, was a bestseller and in 1974 turned into a movie. And while critics have questioned the scale of his accomplishments— partly because of the extensive outside assistance he received, and partly because his wife joined him for short sections of the voyage meaning he was not strictly single-handed throughout—his story has provided inspiration for countless aspiring sailors. All too soon, of course, his record would tumble as ever-younger sailors followed in his wake, but Graham would always have the satisfaction of having been the first genuine youngster to have done it.

Tinkerbelle

WHEN COPY EDITOR ROBERT MANRY SET OFF TO SAIL HIS TINY BOAT TINKERBELLE ACROSS THE ATLANTIC, HE HAD NO IDEA HE WOULD BECOME HIS NEWSPAPER'S BIGGEST STORY. NEITHER CAN HE HAVE IMAGINED THAT WITHIN A FEW YEARS OF ACHIEVING HIS DREAM, HE WOULD LOSE EVERYTHING.

JOURNEY: Falmouth, Massachusetts, to Falmouth, UK
BOAT NAME: *Tinkerbelle*
CAPTAIN: Robert Manry
DATE: 1965
DISTANCE: 3,200 nautical miles (5,900km)

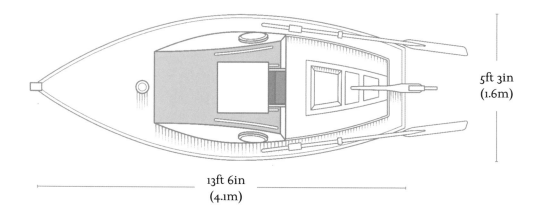

5ft 3in
(1.6m)

13ft 6in
(4.1m)

LENGTH: 13ft 6in (4.1m)
BEAM: 5ft 3in (1.6m)
DRAFT: 2ft (60cm)
DISPLACEMENT: 380lb (172kg)

DATE BUILT: *ca.*1928
RIG: Sloop
CREW: 1

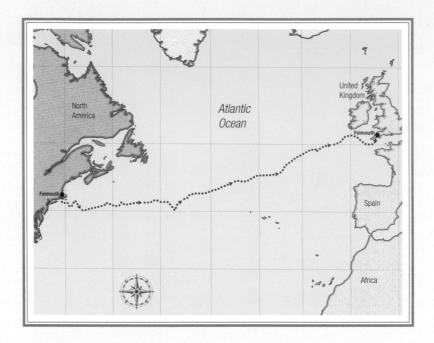

An Ocean Scoop
Tinkerbelle

★ ★ ★

THERE WAS ALMOST NOBODY THERE to say goodbye to Robert Manry when he set off from Falmouth, Massachusetts, on June 1, 1965 in his diminutive boat—just his wife Virginia, his brother-in-law, and the harbormaster. He hadn't told anyone apart from his close family about his crazy plan but, just before pushing off, he handed the harbormaster a letter to post. It was addressed to the *Plain Dealer* newspaper, where Manry was copy editor, and told them his plan to sail the Atlantic to Falmouth, England, on *Tinkerbelle*—at 13ft 6in (4.1m), the smallest boat to make the 3,200-mile (5,900km) voyage at that time. Once the paper's editor got over the shock, he started running articles about Manry and his family, even publishing a letter Manry had handed to a passing ship mid-Atlantic. No editor worth his salt would miss such a scoop.

Born and educated in India—his father had taught at Ewing College in the Himalayas—Manry was a conscientious objector and then a photographer during World War II. Back in the USA, he reported for various papers in Ohio and Pennsylvania before getting a staff job on the *Plain Dealer* in Cleveland. It was while reading the paper's classified ads that he spotted a Whitecap dinghy for sale for $160 and promptly bought it the following morning. It was the kind of boat you might take for an afternoon sail on the lake, but Manry built a cabin over the front and a cockpit in the back, and in 1964 surprised everyone by setting off on a 200-mile (370km) cruise down Lake Erie. That winter, he started talking about crossing the Atlantic with a friend and, when the friend backed out, decided to do the trip on his own.

In a country thirsty for good news, an ordinary American setting off on a daring adventure was a huge hit and Manry became a celebrity on both sides of the Atlantic. So newsworthy was he that a TV crew hired a boat to intercept him 300 miles (555km) from land to out-scoop their rivals. By the time Manry arrived in Falmouth after 58 days at sea, a crowd of 50,000 and 300 boats had gathered to cheer him in. The scenes were repeated when Manry returned to New York, where he appeared on several chat shows, and in his hometown of Willowick, Ohio. For the next few years, Manry rode the wave of fame, appearing in *Life* magazine, giving speeches, and writing a book. But the good times were soon to end. In 1969, Virginia was killed in a freak car accident. Manry married one of her friends the following year, but within a few weeks he, too, had died of a heart attack. It was a tragic end to a great story.

Hōkūle'a

HOW DID THE INDIGENOUS PEOPLE OF POLYNESIA ORIGINALLY MIGRATE TO SUCH ISOLATED ISLANDS, THOUSANDS OF MILES OUT AT SEA? DID THEY TRAVEL THERE INTENTIONALLY OR WERE THEY BLOWN THERE BY THE WIND? FOR ONE GROUP OF MARITIME "INVESTIGATORS," THERE WAS ONLY ONE WAY TO FIND OUT.

JOURNEY: Hawai'i to Tahiti
BOAT NAME: *Hōkūle'a*
CAPTAIN: Kawika Kapahulehua
DATE: 1976
DISTANCE: 2,250 nautical miles (4,170km)

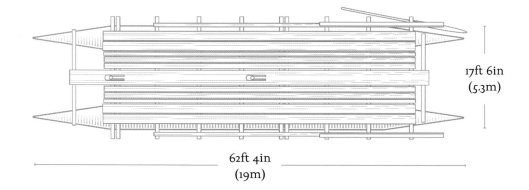

17ft 6in
(5.3m)

62ft 4in
(19m)

LENGTH: 62ft 4in (19m)
BEAM: 17ft 6in (5.3m)
DRAFT: 2ft 6in (76cm)
DISPLACEMENT: 14 tons (12.7 tonnes)

DATE BUILT: 1973–5
RIG: Crab claw
CREW: 15

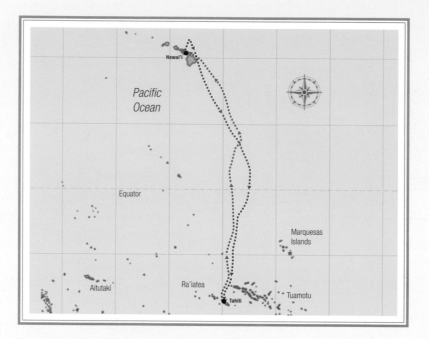

Sailing for History
Hōkūle'a

★ ★ ★

EVER SINCE EUROPEAN EXPLORERS first came across Polynesia in the 16th century and found people living on its isolated islands, the issue of how these people came to be there has perplexed travelers and scientists alike. In 1595, the Portuguese navigator Pedro Fernandes de Queirós concluded there must be a landmass farther south from which they had migrated, while in 1722 the Dutch explorer Jacob Roggeveen suggested that they had descended from Adam. More recently, Thor Heyerdahl proposed that they crossed from South America on rafts, while in 1957 Andrew Sharp revived a theory that they had drifted across the Pacific by accident, driven from one island to the next through poor navigation and seamanship.

All these theories shared two fundamental assumptions: that the Polynesian indigenous craft, with their fragile-looking outriggers and strange clawlike sails, weren't capable of sailing hundreds of miles against the prevailing winds and currents, and that local inhabitants didn't have the navigational know-how to undertake such journeys intentionally. After all, European explorers relied on sturdy ships and all manner of sophisticated navigation instruments to sail across oceans, so how could the Polynesians achieve the same with such primitive craft?

Then another argument emerged in 1973 when a group of "nautically-minded investigators" formed the Polynesian Voyaging Society to raise funds to build a large, traditional canoe to sail from Hawai'i to Tahiti — 2,000 miles (3,700km) south and 500 miles (930km) east (i.e. against the prevailing wind and currents). Although the boat wasn't built using traditional methods and materials, the design was closely based on traditional craft, including anachronistic features such as the narrow beam and those strange clawlike sails Hōkūle'a left Hawai'i on May 1, 1976, under the guidance of her navigator, Mau Piailug. Using the rising points of various stars, along with observations of the sun, moon, and ocean swells, he navigated the ship all the way to Tahiti without any modern instruments.

Which is why, when Hōkūle'a arrived in Tahiti 34 days after leaving Hawai'i, she was greeted by an ecstatic crowd of 17,000 people—more than half the island's population. They knew that two of the foundation stones of the hated "accidental drift" theory had been soundly crushed and that a large chunk of Polynesian history had been reclaimed.

Iduna

Ellen MacArthur would become famous for crying as she climbed the rigging of her state-of-the-art racing yacht and, later, for breaking the round-the-world speed record. But, before either of those events, there was Iduna, the 21ft (6.3m) cruising boat she sailed around Britain when she was just a teenager.

JOURNEY: Around Britain, via the Caledonian Canal
BOAT NAME: *Iduna*
CAPTAIN: Ellen MacArthur
DATE: 1995
DISTANCE: 1,500 nautical miles (2,800km)

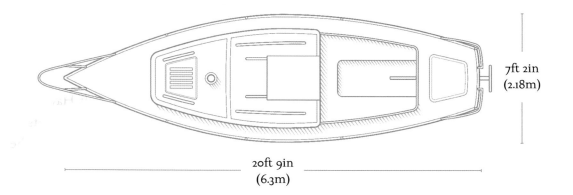

7ft 2in
(2.18m)

20ft 9in
(6.3m)

LENGTH: 20ft 9in (6.3m)
BEAM: 7ft 2in (2.18m)
DRAFT: 3ft (90cm)
DISPLACEMENT: 1 ton (0.9 tonnes)

DATE BUILT: *ca.*1970s
RIG: Sloop
CREW: 1

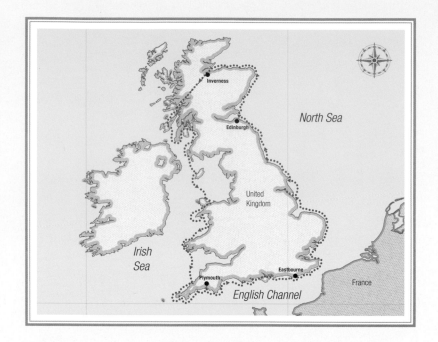

The Making of Ellen
Iduna

★ ★ ★

THERE WERE SEVERAL MOMENTS of epiphany during Ellen MacArthur's childhood that led, with seeming inevitability, to her becoming a sailing icon. The first was when she went for her first sail, aged five, with her Aunt Thea. "We went completely out of sight of land, and for the first time in my life I felt totally free," she later wrote. "I was hooked." After that, she saved all her school dinner money so that, aged 13, she could buy her first boat. Another transformative moment was her first overnight trip, crossing the North Sea, again with her aunt: "... sailing through the sunset and then the sunrise the following day was a whole new adventure. There was a feeling of constancy and endlessness about this kind of sailing. Why should we stop, why do we need to pull into port each night, why can't we carry on further?"

But it was spotting *Iduna*, just after recovering from a serious bout of glandular fever, which set the course of her life for good. "There she was, stern towards me like a scruffy heap. Her rudder was askew and one of her backstays hung lifelessly beside her mast." Most people would have run a mile, but for Ellen, "It was love at first sight." It was only several months later, just before her first meeting with a potential sponsor, that she decided what she was going to do with the boat: sail around Britain single-handed. With typical professionalism, she planned the journey meticulously, breaking the 1,500-mile (2,800km) journey into five stages, each made up of five or six shorter legs. As she left Hull on June 1, 1995, she had a clear sense of destiny. "It was as if I'd left every part of my life up until that moment behind me on the dockside," she wrote. "Ahead was an unknown future, and suspended between the two were *Iduna* and I, waiting for the past to disappear over the horizon."

Her voyage around Britain was successful though relatively uneventful: she survived storms, didn't have appendicitis, saw dolphins and phosphorescence, and made lifelong friends at every turn (everyone loves Ellen). Perhaps most importantly, though, she discovered she loved being alone at sea. The experience of that voyage would feed into everything she did thereafter, and very soon her life would be utterly transformed. Three years later, she would enter the legendary Route du Rhum race, winning her class, and three years after that she would fulfill her dream and sail around the world, finishing second in the Vendée Globe race. Ellen MacArthur, the sailing legend, had been born.

Firecrest

HE'S ONE OF FRANCE'S SAILING HEROES AND ONLY THE THIRD MAN TO SAIL AROUND THE WORLD SINGLE-HANDED, YET ALAIN GERBAULT'S REPUTATION IS CONSTANTLY UNDER ATTACK WITH ACCUSATIONS OF HIM HAVING A POP-STAR ATTITUDE LONG BEFORE POP STARS WERE EVEN INVENTED.

ROUTE: Cannes to Le Havre, France, via the world
BOAT NAME: *Firecrest*
CAPTAIN: Alain Gerbault
DATE: 1923–29
DISTANCE: 40,000 nautical miles (74,000km)

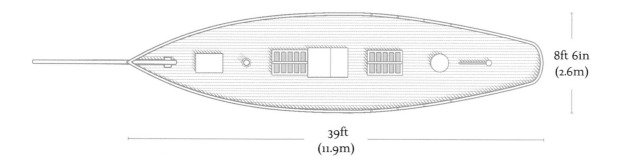

8ft 6in
(2.6m)

39ft
(11.9m)

LENGTH: 39ft (11.9m)
BEAM: 8ft 6in (2.6m)
DRAFT: 7ft (2.1m)
DISPLACEMENT: 11.65 tons (10.6 tonnes)

DATE BUILT: 1892
RIG: Gaff cutter (Bermudan after 1924)
CREW: 1

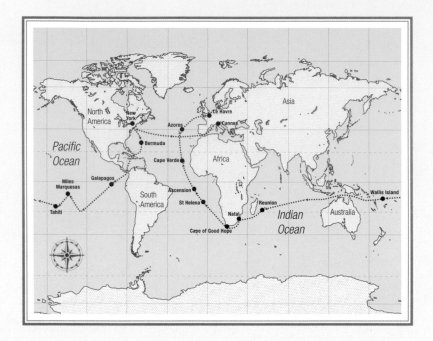

The Troubled Hero
Firecrest

★ ★ ★

WHEN A MAN WINS MEDALS flying planes in World War I, becomes a top tennis player, sails around the world single-handed, is awarded the Légion d'Honneur, and writes bestselling books about his experiences, he might be forgiven for thinking his reputation was secure. Not so Alain Gerbault, whose achievements were undermined by his personal behavior.

Born to an affluent family in northwest France, Gerbault trained as a civil engineer and, in 1914, volunteered for the French Air Force. He was rapidly promoted and won several medals, including the Croix de Guerre. At the war's end, he embarked on a successful tennis career, rising to become the 5th-best French player in 1923. At the peak of his career, however, he decided to fulfill a childhood cream and go sailing. The boat he chose was both strikingly beautiful and completely inappropriate: the 39ft (11.9m) *Firecrest*, designed for racing by British designer Dixon Kemp and, to an experienced eye, far too "nervy" for his intended voyage.

Gerbault set off from Cannes in April 1923, stopping at Gibraltar to make repairs, before sailing across the Atlantic to New York in 101 days to become the first man to make such a single-handed crossing from east to west. He was greeted with great acclaim in the USA, and popped back to France to play some more tennis, before resuming his journey the following year. The rest of his circumnavigation continued to be a catalog of accidents, with constant storm damage and repeated stops for repairs, culminating in the boat losing its keel on a reef in Tahiti. Such was his celebrity by then, however, that the French Navy was called in to fix the boat. Gerbault limped back to France in July 1929 and, despite criticism that he had spent more time repairing his boat than actually sailing her, was awarded the Légion d'Honneur.

He donated *Firecrest* to the nation but the boat sank while being towed to a new mooring. Undaunted, Gerbault built another boat which, with characteristic modesty, he named after himself. He sailed *Alain Gerbault* back to Polynesia in 1932 and became a vocal defender of indigenous rights—although rumors persist that he abused young men while living there. Already under fire from sailing experts, his reputation suffered another blow when he supported the Nazi-backed Vichy government in 1940 and had to flee French Polynesia. He ended up in East Timor, where he died of fever in December 1941. His remains were disinterred and reburied in Bora Bora in 1947, according to his dying wishes.

Squeak

When Stephen Ladd got fed up with his sensible job as a city planner, he designed and built a 12ft (3.7m) boat to take him on a grand adventure. His diminutive boat was to be his home for the next three years, while he traveled across the Americas.

ROUTE: Montana to Florida, via New Orleans, Panama, Colombia, and Trinidad
BOAT NAME: *Squeak*
CAPTAIN: Stephen Ladd
DATE: 1990–93
DISTANCE: 15,000 nautical miles (27,780km)

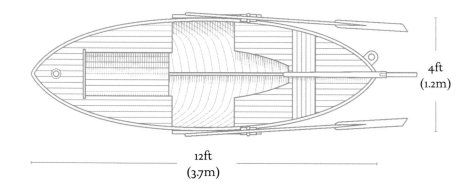

4ft
(1.2m)

12ft
(3.7m)

LENGTH: 12ft (3.7m)
BEAM: 4ft (1.2m)
DRAFT: 8in (20cm)
DISPLACEMENT: 250lb (113kg)

DATE BUILT: 1990
RIG: Yawl
CREW: 1

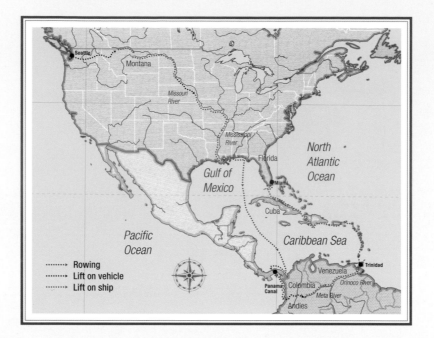

A Peapod with a Mission
Squeak

★ ★ ★

SHE LOOKS LIKE A MINIATURE lifeboat. Or a decked-over rowing dinghy. Or an overgrown peapod sculpted out of wood. But whatever you might think about *Squeak*, remember this: she has traveled 15,000 miles (27,780km)—down rivers, up mountains (on the backs of trucks), and across oceans—almost half that distance under her own steam. For three years she was the only home of her owner, Stephen Ladd, who took her from the northernmost part of the USA to South America, over the Andes, and back home to Florida on his own. Not bad for a 12ft (3.7m) boat designed and built by a complete amateur.

It all started in 1987, when Ladd, a city planner in Seattle, dreamt of recreating the freewheeling lifestyle of his youth. After reading dozens of books on naval architecture, he designed a 30ft (9.1m) boat for him and his girlfriend. Realizing their relationship might not last, he halved the size of the boat to 15ft (4.5m), then reduced it again to 12ft (3.7m) to achieve the 250lb (113kg) maximum weight he had set himself. The result was a half-decked, double-ended cockleshell with a cabin long enough to lie in, a surfboard sail at either end, and two oars to propel her in light airs. Ladd built her in cold-molded wood on the terrace of his apartment in downtown Seattle, and named her *Squeak* "after a dearly departed cat." Total cost: $2,000.

On August 11, 1990, he set off from the northernmost, navigable tributary of the Mississippi: a mountain stream in Montana, half a mile from the Canadian border and about 4,000ft (1,219m) above sea level. From there, he rowed and sailed down most of the Missouri and Mississippi Rivers (hiring a car for one section to avoid the onset of winter) before hitching a ride on a cargo ship across the Gulf of Mexico to the Panama Canal. Sailing along the Pacific Coast, he nearly drowned when his boat filled up with water while he was sleeping and he woke up to find himself paddling in the sea at night, surrounded by lightning. After hitching a ride by truck over the Andes, he rowed 600 miles (1,100km) down the Meta and Orinoco Rivers, escorted part of the way by pink dolphins, and emerged in the Atlantic Ocean near Trinidad. Finally, he cruised northward through the Caribbean—capsizing, being arrested, and falling in and out of love along the way—before reaching Florida on May 16, 1993, just before his 40th birthday. Some 15,000 miles (27,780km), 19 countries, and three years later, Ladd's faith in his design was vindicated—whatever it might look like.

America

THE YACHT AMERICA CAME TO BRITAIN TO SHOW OFF US BOATBUILDING EXPERTISE AT THE GREAT EXHIBITION OF 1851. SHE ENDED UP THRASHING THE BRITS ON THEIR HOME TURF AND THEREBY LAUNCHING THE OLDEST CONTINUOUSLY RACED SPORTING EVENT IN HISTORY.

JOURNEY: Around the Isle of Wight

BOAT NAME: *America*

CAPTAIN: Dick Brown

DATE: 1851

DISTANCE: 53 nautical miles (98km)

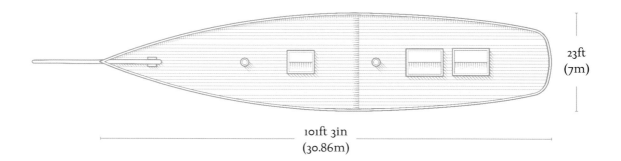

101ft 3in
(30.86m)

23ft
(7m)

LENGTH: 101ft 3in (30.86m)

BEAM: 23ft (7m)

DRAFT: 10ft 11in (3.3m)

DISPLACEMENT: 190.7 tons (173 tonnes)

DATE BUILT: 1851

RIG: Schooner

CREW: 21

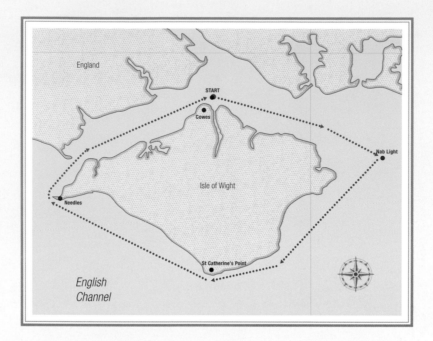

England

START

Cowes

Needles

Nab Light

Isle of Wight

St Catherine's Point

English
Channel

The First America's Cup
America

★ ★ ★

THE INDUSTRIAL REVOLUTION WAS in full swing when Prince Albert gave the go-ahead for the Great Exhibition at Crystal Palace in 1851. The event was to showcase the ingenuity of British designers and manufacturers, as well as its colonies and 44 "foreign states." The fledgling state of America brought a grain reaper, Colt revolvers, and a "patent double grand piano." It also brought a yacht: the 101ft (30.8m) *America*, built by a consortium of East Coast businessmen under the aegis of the New York Yacht Club. The new schooner was dramatically different from most British yachts of the period, which were "cod's head and mackerel tail"-shaped, based on the idea of punching a hole through the water, which the rest of the hull slipped through with minimal resistance. By contrast, *America* had a fine bow, broadening to a wide beam amidships—more like the modern racing boats of today.

When *America* turned up in Cowes on July 31, 1851, at the invitation of the Royal Yacht Squadron, she was greeted with skepticism mixed with a great deal of curiosity. The *Illustrated London News* postulated "she is artistic, although rather a violation of the old established ideas of naval architecture," while one member of the RYS declared, "If she's right we must all be wrong." The local yachtsmen were initially reluctant to race against *America*, having heard reports she had thrashed a British boat on her way to Cowes, but a race was eventually organized around the Isle of Wight. The prize was an ornate silver cup worth 100 guineas.

Fourteen boats turned up on August 22, ranging in size from the 47-ton (42.7-tonne) *Aurora* to the 393-ton (357-tonne) schooner *Brilliant*. As the start gun was fired at 10 a.m., *America* got off to a slow start, but she had soon caught up with the rest and by the first mark was in fifth place. The traditional course was around the Nab Buoy, but this wasn't specified on the race instructions, so *America* took the shorter route to the next mark and gained the lead. She stayed in front for the rest of the race, and when the wind died on the last leg and the valiant little *Aurora* started catching up, *America* was too far ahead and crossed the finish line at 8:37 p.m., eight minutes ahead of her much smaller rival. Only three other boats finished the race within the allocated time. *America* had trounced the pride of British yachting and laid the foundation for what has become the longest-running sporting event in history: the America's Cup. Britain have never succeeded in regaining the "auld mug," despite 19 attempts.

Guppy

Most parents would be horrified if their 16-year-old daughter told them she wanted to sail around the world single-handed. Not Laura Dekker's parents. They were fully behind her—but first they would have to navigate their way through the Dutch courts.

JOURNEY: Gibraltar to St Martin, via Panama Canal, around the world
BOAT NAME: *Guppy*
CAPTAIN: Laura Dekker
DATE: 2010–12
DISTANCE: 27,000 nautical miles (50,000km)

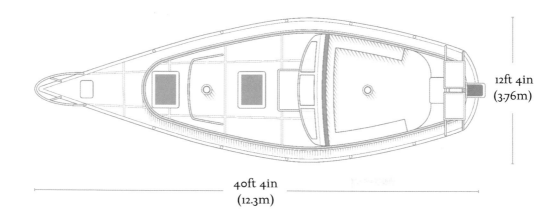

12ft 4in
(3.76m)

40ft 4in
(12.3m)

LENGTH: 40ft 4in (12.3m)
BEAM: 12ft 4in (3.76m)
DRAFT: 6ft 3in (1.9m)
DISPLACEMENT: 12.3 tons (11.2 tonnes)

DATE BUILT: 1978
RIG: Ketch
CREW: 1

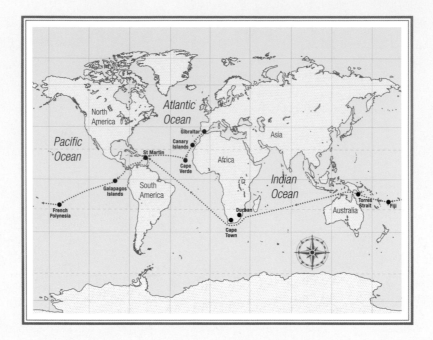

A Race Against Time
Guppy

★ ★ ★

WHEN 17-YEAR-OLD MIKE PERHAM sailed into Portsmouth in August 2009 to become the youngest person to sail around the world single-handed, he set the clock ticking for a generation of sailors determined to beat his record. First was Australian Jessica Watson, aged 16, whose loop around the Southern Hemisphere wasn't deemed long enough to be regarded as proper circumnavigation. Next up, American Abby Sunderland had to give up when her boat was dismasted in the Indian Ocean. That should have left it wide open for Dutch sailor Laura Dekker, who was barely 14 in August 2009 when she announced she was planning the trip—if only the Dutch authorities hadn't intervened. When the country's child services got wind of Dekker's plans, they applied for shared custody and forbade the voyage—even though she had the backing of her parents. The legal battle was especially agonizing for Dekker, who knew that her chances of beating Perham's record grew smaller with each passing month.

Despite her age, Dekker was an experienced sailor. Born in New Zealand while her parents were sailing around the world, she lived on boats until she was five. Aged six she learned to sail in an Optimist dinghy and was soon helming on her own. By ten she had graduated to a Hurley 700 pocket cruiser, which she sailed around Friesland with her dog Spot for company. In spring 2009, Dekker sailed single-handed across the Channel to Lowestoft. Unimpressed with the 13-year-old's achievement, the British authorities took her into care and called her father to collect her. He initially refused, saying she was capable of sailing home on her own, before eventually capitulating and flying over—only to let her sail back alone anyway.

The legal wrangles over Dekker's planned circumnavigation delayed her departure by a year and turned her into a *cause célèbre* as the world's media debated the extent to which the state should interfere to protect a child from danger. Even when a Dutch court finally handed custody back to her parents in August 2010, Dekker was unable to start her circumnavigation in Dutch waters as the boat she was sailing was over 7m (23ft)—the maximum size under-16s are allowed to skipper in Holland. Instead, her father accompanied her to Gibraltar from where, on August 21, 2010, her attempt at the record officially began. After several stops along the way, 518 days later Dekker arrived at St Martin in the Caribbean to become the youngest person to sail around the world single-handed. She was 16 years and 123 days old.

Bluenose

Nearly a hundred years after she was launched, the mighty Bluenose still features on Canadian coins, a symbol of national pride. So why did the famous schooner, unbeaten in her own lifetime, end her days wrecked on a coral reef in the Caribbean? And why is the 1963 replica, built to exactly the same plans, not quite as fast as the original?

JOURNEY: Race course off Halifax, Nova Scotia
BOAT NAME: *Bluenose*
CAPTAIN: Angus Walters
DATE: 1921–38
DISTANCE: 39.5 nautical miles (73km)

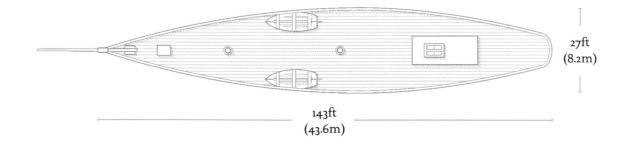

143ft
(43.6m)

27ft
(8.2m)

LENGTH: 143ft (43.6m)
BEAM: 27ft (8.2m)
DRAFT: 15ft 10in (4.83m)
DISPLACEMENT: 319 ton (289 tonnes)

DATE BUILT: 1921
RIG: Schooner
CREW: 22

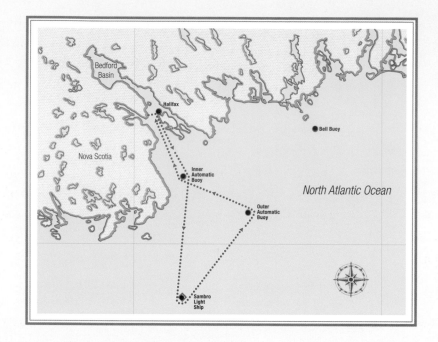

The Other America's Cup
Bluenose

★ ★ ★

THE GRAND BANKS FISHING SCHOONERS were famously hardy, spending up to two months working at sea in all weathers to bring home their catch. No surprise then that when the 1920 America's Cup was postponed because of winds of more than 23 knots (43km/h)—a mere breeze by Grand Banks standards—most of those fishermen howled with laughter. Their

Christiania

Colin Archer rescue boats were famous for going out in any weather and saving fishing boats off Norway's rugged coast. The design inspired countless imitations, which today continue to sail around the world. So when one of these historic vessels went down in the North Sea for no obvious reason, everyone wanted to know: why did Christiania sink? First, however, they had to find her.

JOURNEY: Oslo to 57° 48' N, 7° 39' E
BOAT NAME: *Christiania*
CAPTAIN: Johan Petersen
DATE: 1997
DISTANCE: 200 nautical miles (370km)

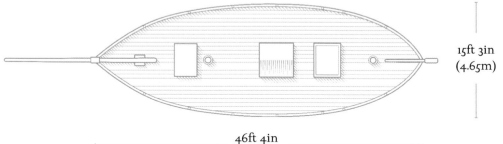

15ft 3in
(4.65m)

46ft 4in
(14.12m)

LENGTH: 46ft 4in (14.12m)
BEAM: 15ft 3in (4.65m)
DRAFT: 7ft 10in (2.4m)
DISPLACEMENT: 33.6 tons (30.5 tonnes)

DATE BUILT: 1895
RIG: Gaff ketch
CREW: 6

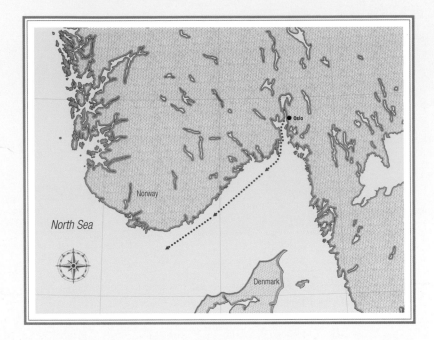

Rescuing the Rescuer

Christiania

★ ★ ★

CHRISTIANIA WAS ON A ROUTINE PASSAGE across the North Sea from Oslo to London when, 15 miles (28.3km) off the southern tip of Norway, the unthinkable happened. As she fell off a wave, her planking opened up and she started taking on water. Despite pumping for three hours with four bilge pumps, skipper Johan Petersen and his five crew couldn't stem the flow and sent out a mayday. But even when the rescue helicopter arrived and lowered two diesel-powered pumps with a combined capacity of 370 gallons (1,400 liters) per minute, it wasn't enough to save the yacht. Four hours after the leak started, Johan and his crew scrambled into a life raft and watched their beloved family yacht slide, stern first, into the sea.

In the usual run of things, the story would have ended there. *Christiania* had sunk in 1,600ft (500m) of water, and the chances of rescuing her from that depth seemed pretty remote. But a few weeks later, the Petersens returned with a remote-operated vehicle (ROV) and managed to locate the boat at 57° 48' N, 7° 39' E. Unbelievably, Christiania was sitting quite comfortably upright in the mud, intact apart from some damage to the rudder. "She looked just fine, sitting on the mud bottom," said Johan. "She had just waited."

A few months later the Petersens were back with a 300ft (100m) oil-exploration vessel "loaned" by an oil exploration company. After 17 hours' painstaking work, a custom-made sling was attached to the yacht using a remotely operated vehicle, and she was lifted bow-first out of the mud and then leveled up for her journey back to the surface. Finally, on May 3, 1999, 20 months after she had sunk, the top of *Christiania's* mast emerged, followed by the rest of her seaweed-encrusted rig. It was a spectacular sight, as the waterlogged vessel emerged from the deep like a great sea monster. Once the water had been pumped out, she floated perfectly and was towed to Mandal, Norway, where the long process of restoration would begin.

But first, the Petersens had to address the question every traditional boat owner wanted answered: why had *Christiania* sunk in the first place? Close inspection revealed that one of the timbers under the mast had a butt joint which, with age, had worked loose and pushed open the planking. It was a small mistake on the part of the yacht's builders, probably due to a shortage of good oak, but 102 years later it was enough to sink the boat.

Kon-Tiki

THOR HEYERDAHL MADE HIS NAME BY PROVING A SIMPLE RAFT COULD SAIL 4,300 MILES (8,000KM) ACROSS THE PACIFIC, CONTRARY TO CONVENTIONAL THINKING. HIS GREAT ADVENTURE NOT ONLY FAILED TO CONVINCE THE SCIENTISTS OF HIS DAY BUT, IN HINDSIGHT, WAS SKEWED BY A DISTINCTLY WESTERN BIAS. SO DID NORWAY'S MAVERICK ETHNOLOGIST MISS THE POINT?

JOURNEY: Lima, Peru, to Raroia, Tuamotus
BOAT NAME: *Kon-Tiki*
CAPTAIN: Thor Heyerdahl
DATE: 1949
DISTANCE: 4,300 nautical miles (8,000km)

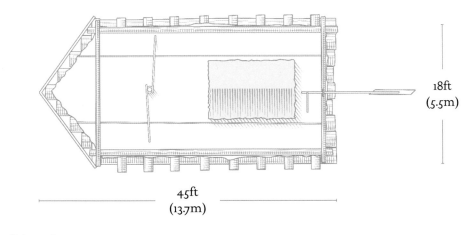

18ft
(5.5m)

45ft
(13.7m)

LENGTH: 45ft (13.7m)
BEAM: 18ft (5.5m)
HEIGHT: 4ft 10in (1.47m) (bottom to deck)
DISPLACEMENT: 16.8 tons (15.2 tonnes)

DATE BUILT: 1949
RIG: Square sail
CREW: 6

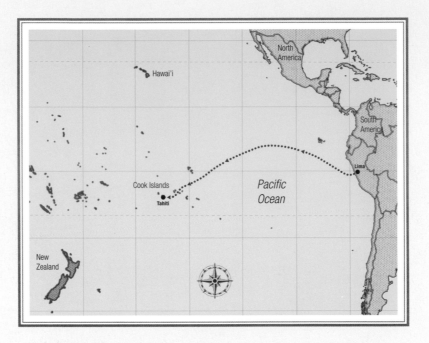

East of the Sun, West of the Moon
Kon-Tiki

★ ★ ★

THOR HEYERDAHL AND HIS WIFE were living on an island in the South Pacific, collecting specimens of flora and fauna, when he had a heretical idea. He had noticed how the wind always battered the east side of the island, not the west, and how native South American plants such as sweet potatoes grew on the island, even though South America lay far away, response was to set up a "race for real sailors:" the International Fisherman's Trophy, to be raced by working boats that had fished the Grand Banks for at least one season. Essentially, that meant a race between American and Canadian schooners, mostly from Gloucester and Lunenburg, which had long had informal races to see who would get to the fisheries first.

The first contest, off Halifax in October 1920, was convincingly won by the Americans, who took the silver cup and C$4,000 prize money home to Gloucester—much to the annoyance of the Canadians. They consoled themselves that Canadian schooners usually spent longer at sea and needed bigger holds and were less streamlined than their American counterparts. But within a few weeks of losing the first event, a consortium of Halifax businessmen had commissioned plans for a new schooner designed specifically to win the race—although of course when she wasn't racing she would have to work as a fishing boat, as per the rules.

The 143ft- (43.6m-) long *Bluenose* was launched less than four months later and looked decidedly more streamlined than her Canadian predecessors. Designed and built by a Canadian team and constructed of Canadian timber (except the masts, which came from Oregon), she soon proved her worth when, after a season fishing on the Grand Banks, she won her first Fisherman's Trophy in October 1921. She repeated the win in 1922 and 1923— while at the same time bringing home record catches of fish—and won every contest she entered until the final Fisherman's Trophy in 1938. She soon became a symbol of Canadian pride, attending the Chicago World's Fair and King George V's Silver Jubilee, and featuring on the Canadian 50-cent stamp and dime coin (where she still remains). By this time, however, she was obsolete as a fishing boat and was sold off to carry cargo across the Caribbean, until she was finally wrecked on a reef off Haiti in 1946. Less than 20 years later, a replica was built costing nearly ten times as much but was never quite as fast as the original, despite being built to the same plans. Even from the bottom of the sea, the *Bluenose* legend lives on.

across 4,300 miles (8,000km) of empty sea. Surely if sweet potatoes could migrate from the east, then people could too? It was an idea that went against contemporary scientific theories, which suggested the Pacific islands had been settled by people migrating gradually, island by island, from the west. While the trade winds undoubtedly blew from east to west, critics argued there were no native craft capable of making a 4,300-mile (8,000km) ocean crossing in 500AD or even 1000AD, as suggested by Heyerdahl.

There was only one way to prove his hypothesis, and so in 1947 Heyerdahl flew to Peru and started building a traditional raft, using only tools and materials available to indigenous people of that period. Nine enormous balsa logs were lashed together using hemp rope, and a square sail was rigged for downwind sailing. A simple bamboo cabin covered with banana leaves provided the only shelter. The raft carried modern navigation equipment, including radios, sextant, and charts, but had only minimal steerage. It was named *Kon-Tiki* after an ancient Inca sun god who was said to have traveled to the west.

Surviving largely on caught fish, Heyerdahl and his five crew (plus one parrot, lost in a storm) survived 101 days at sea, before crashing onto a reef on Raroia, an island 500 miles (930km) north of Tahiti. Heyerdahl had proven such a voyage was possible but not that it was probable, and most scientists continued to believe migration from the west was more likely. What's more, Heyerdahl's thinking revealed a fundamental Western prejudice. Just like his opponents, he assumed the Polynesian craft were incapable of sailing to windward and that native people were incapable of navigating with deliberate intent and had merely been blown from island to island at the whim of the elements. It wasn't until 1976 that the Hawai'ian canoe *Hōkule'a* proved that this theory of "accidental drift" was not only patronizing but wrong. Traditional Polynesian craft could both sail into the wind and navigate from island to island using traditional methods. Heyerdahl's great adventure had been flawed from the outset.

Fram

THE RACE WAS ON TO BE THE FIRST PERSON TO REACH THE NORTH POLE WHEN NORWEGIAN EXPLORER FRIDTJOF NANSEN CAME UP WITH AN EXTRAORDINARY PLAN. RATHER THAN STRUGGLE ACROSS THE ICE WITH TONS OF FOOD OR EQUIPMENT, HE WOULD BUILD A BOAT THAT WOULD BE CARRIED TO THE POLE BY THE ICE ITSELF. SOUND TOO GOOD TO BE TRUE? NANSEN WOULD PROBABLY AGREE. . .

JOURNEY: Vardø, to Skjervøy, Norway, via the Arctic'
BOAT NAME: *Fram*
CAPTAIN: Fridtjof Nansen
DATE: 1893–96
DISTANCE: 54,000 nautical miles (100,000km)

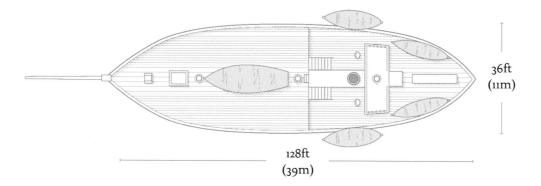

36ft
(11m)

128ft
(39m)

LENGTH: 128ft (39m)
BEAM: 36ft (11m)
DRAFT: 17ft (5.2m)
DISPLACEMENT: 402 tons (365 tonnes)

DATE BUILT: 1892
RIG: Three-masted schooner
CREW: 13

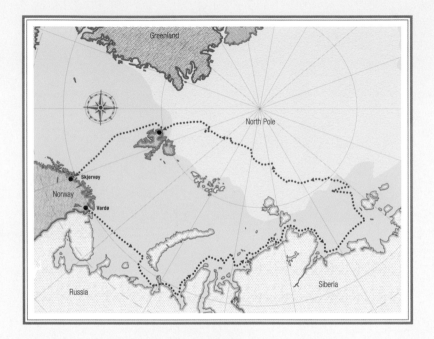

Furthest North
Fram

★ ★ ★

IT WAS A CRAZY IDEA: to deliberately sail a boat into the ice and let the movement of the ice floes "drift" her to the North Pole. All the experts, including the Royal Geographical Society, agreed the proposal was at best foolish and at worse suicidal. But Fridtjof Nansen was having none of it. He had read reports of the SS *Jeanette*, which had become icebound north of

Siberia and drifted across the Arctic for 21 months before being crushed. Three years later, debris from her wreck had turned up in Greenland, 29,000 miles (54,000km) from where she had gone down. To Nansen, this proved that the Arctic ice moved in a westerly direction. All you had to do was build a boat strong enough to withstand the pressure of the ice, and wait.

To prove his theory, Nansen built an extraordinary ship, with a rounded hull and almost non-existent keel, designed to rise to the surface of the ice rather than be crushed by it. Massively constructed from solid oak and greenheart, *Fram* was unlike any boat built before or since. Nansen and his 12 crew set sail in the summer of 1893 and headed toward the Siberian Islands, north of Russia. There they duly drove *Fram* into the ice, and waited. As the ice closed in, the ship shook and groaned and was lifted bodily out of the water. Each time, it sounded as if she was about to be crushed, but each time she survived and was released back into the sea—exactly as Nansen had intended.

His theory of polar drift was proven correct, too, as the ship edged northward and westwards, albeit painfully slowly. After nearly two years, it became clear they were going to miss the North Pole, and Nansen decided to make a dash for it by sledge, accompanied by one crew. It was to prove a miserable journey, as the two men struggled against the odds before eventually turning back at 86° 14' N—the farthest north anyone had ever been. It took them another 15 months to return home to Norway, including nine months endured in a stone shelter in Franz Josef Land. *Fram*, meanwhile, continued on her journey, passing just 17 miles (31km) south of Nansen's most northerly point, and re-emerged near Spitsbergen after three years in the ice. Nearly 20 years later, she would be used for another extraordinary voyage, when Roald Amundsen became the first man to reach the South Pole. What was once regarded as a mad idea became a national institution when *Fram* was preserved in her own museum in 1935, where she continues to astound.

Gjøa

THE SEARCH FOR THE ELUSIVE NORTHWEST PASSAGE OBSESSED THE WESTERN WORLD FOR CENTURIES AND CLAIMED THE LIVES OF HUNDRED OF SAILORS—UNTIL 1905, WHEN A YOUNG NORWEGIAN EXPLORER STRAPPED FOR CASH SET OFF IN AN OLD FISHING BOAT WITH SIX CREW AND 20 DOGS. HIS NAME WAS ROALD AMUNDSEN, AND HE WOULD GO ON TO CHANGE THE FACE OF POLAR EXPLORATION.

JOURNEY: Norway to Alaska, via the Northwest Passage
BOAT NAME: *Gjøa*
CAPTAIN: Roald Amundsen
DATE: 1903–06
DISTANCE: 900 nautical miles (1,700km)

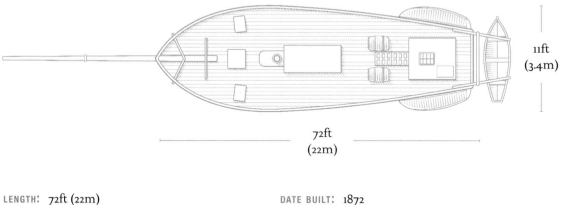

11ft
(3.4m)

72ft
(22m)

LENGTH: 72ft (22m)
BEAM: 11ft (3.4m)
DRAFT: 3ft (1m)
DISPLACEMENT: 52.6 tons (47.8 tonnes)

DATE BUILT: 1872
RIG: Gaff cutter
CREW: 7

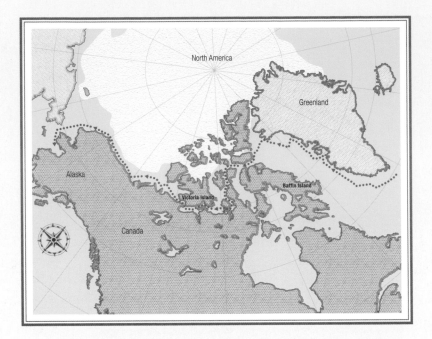

The Search for the Northwest Passage
Gjøa

★ ★ ★

AT MIDNIGHT ON JUNE 6, 1903, the crew of a 72ft (22m) former herring boat moored in Christiania harbor slipped her lines and motored down the Oslofjord. The leader, Roald Amundsen, had blown his inheritance buying and equipping *Gjøa* and had borrowed money to finance the trip. But, before even leaving, the sponsors were baying for their money back.

Like many men of his time, Amundsen had become obsessed with finding the Northwest Passage, which was thought to join the Atlantic and Pacific Oceans via the Arctic. In the days before the Panama Canal was built, it was assumed that if such a passage could be found, ships would be able to cross from one side of America to the other without going around Cape Horn. Since the Franklin Expedition had vanished without trace in 1845, complete with her captain and 128 crew, countless expeditions had set out to discover what had become of them and find the elusive passage—doubtless encouraged by the British government's offer of a £10,000 reward for the discovery of either.

Amundsen's expedition might have been operating on a shoestring, but its modest size was to prove its greatest asset. The young explorer had a hunch the passage lay farther south than others had tried and, after rounding Baffin Island, headed straight for the south coast of King William Island, where he set up camp in what would become known as Gjoa Haven. There, he and his crew devoted two years to fulfilling the expedition's official purpose: taking meteorological readings and recording the position of the magnetic North Pole (which was, at that time, about 1,000 miles (1800km) away from the geographical North Pole).

Finally, in August 1905, they broke camp and set sail on the most risky part of their voyage: the Simpson Strait, which had never been crossed by ship before. *Gjøa*'s relatively small size and shallow draft was a key factor as they passed over this tricky area, sometimes with only inches of water under the keel. Two weeks after leaving King William Island, they spotted a sail ahead of them, and there was only one place a ship could have come from: the Bering Strait at the other end of the Northwest Passage. They had made it. It would take another year for Amundsen and his men to fully extract themselves from the ice and make their way to a hero's welcome in San Francisco. By then, *Gjøa* had no need to sneak out of harbor by dead of night: Amundsen was famous, and his sponsors could be sure of getting their money back.

Glossary

AFT At the back end of the ship

AMIDSHIPS In the middle of the ship

BEAMY Wide

BERMUDAN A triangular mainsail whose front edge is attached to the mast

BILGE Lowest part of the inside of a ship, usually under the cabin sole

BOW The front, or "pointy" end, of a ship

CENTERBOARD A retractable keel projecting under the hull

CHRONOMETER A timepiece with a very accurate mechanism, used for determining longitude

CLINKER Made from wooden planks where the lower edge of each plank overlaps the plank below it

CLIPPER Fast sailing ship used in the nineteenth century for carrying cargo

COCKPIT A sunken area at the back of a boat where the helm and engine controls are usually located

COLD-MOLDED Made from thin layers of wood bent around a mold and glued together

CUTTER A sailboat with a single mast and at least two sails in front of the mast

DECK The upper, horizontal part of the boat's structure

DORY A small boat with flat bottom and straight, flaring sides, native to the east coast of America

DOUBLE-ENDED A hull that is "pointy" at both ends

DRAFT The depth of a ship at its deepest point

DROGUE A long line towed behind a ship to slow it down in a storm

FORE Toward the front of the ship

FRAME The transverse "ribs" of the hull that give a ship its shape and strength.

GAFF A four-sided sail hoisted up the mast on an angled spar that does not overlap the mast

GALLEY A ship's kitchen

GUNWALES The top edge of a ship's hull

HALF-DECKED When a hull is only partially decked over, usually the front half

HELM The wheel or tiller used to steer a ship

HOLD The area of the hull (usually in the middle) used to carry cargo

HULL The main body of a boat

HULL SPEED The theoretical maximum speed of a boat, given by the formula 1.4 x square root of the waterline length (in feet)

ITCHEN FERRY A gaff-rigged boat once used in the Solent area for fishing and ferrying people

JIBE To alter course when sailing downwind, so the wind passes from one side of the mainsail to the other

JURY RIG A temporary mast and sail erected to replace a rig that has broken

KEEL The longitudinal part of the hull, which sticks out from the bottom

KETCH A two-masted sailboat whose back mast is shorter than the front mast and is positioned in front of the helm

KNOCKDOWN When a ship heels over by 90 degrees or more, so that the mast touches the water

KNOT A unit of measure for the speed of a boat, equivalent to 1.15mph (1.85km/h)

LUG A four-sided sail set at an angle on a spar that overlaps the mast

MAINSAIL A large sail set behind the main mast

MAST A large vertical pole to which the sails are attached

OUTRIGGER A float set on a frame that is attached to the side of a boat to increase stability

PERIGUA A narrow boat, native to the Caribbean and usually built entirely or in part from a dugout log.

PITCHPOLE To capsize end over end

PLANING When the front part of a boat rises over its bow wave and glides over the water at great speed

PORT The side of a boat on the left when facing forward

REEF To temporarily reduce the size of a sail, usually due to excessive wind

SCHOONER A sailboat with at least two masts of equal height, or with the mast nearer the stern (back) being the taller

SCUTTLE To deliberately sink a ship by opening seacocks or cutting holes in the bottom

SHARPIE A flat-bottomed sailboat native to the East Coast of America

SKIFF A small rowing boat

SLOOP A sailboat with one mast, setting only one sail forward of the mast

SNEAKBOX A small boat used to hunt birds in inland waters

SPECTRA™ A lightweight, high-strength modern rope

STARBOARD The side of a boat on the right when facing forward

STERN The back, or blunt end, of a boat

TACK Sailing at an angle of less than 90 degrees to the wind, making progress to windward

TILLER A lever used to rotate the rudder and steer the boat

TOPSIDES The part of the hull above the waterline

YAWL A two-masted sailboat whose back mast is shorter than the front mast and is positioned behind the helm

Further Reading

SPRAY
Sailing Alone Around the World
Joshua Slocum (1899)

CENTENNIAL REPUBLIC
Four Months in a Sneakbox
Nathaniel H. Bishop (1879)

PARATII
Between Two Poles
Amyr Klink (1992)
www.amyrklink.com

SWALLOW
Swallows and Amazons
Arthur Ransome (1930)

SUPER SILVER
I Had to Dare
Tom MacClean (1971)
*Salt, Sweat, Tears: The Men Who
Rowed the Oceans*
Adam Rackley (2014)

NOVA ESPERO
Smiths at Sea
Stanley Smith (1951)

HUCK'S RAFT
The Adventures of Huckleberry Finn
Mark Twain (1884)

SUHAILI
A World of My Own
Robin Knox-Johnston (1969)
A Voyage for Madmen

Peter Nichols (2002)
Sailing Solo
Nic Compton (2003)
www.robinknox-johnston.co.uk

SEA SERPENT
www.atlantic-yachtclub.com
/Les-transatlantiques-en-solitaire

PRIDE OF THE THAMES
Three Men in a Boat
Jerome K. Jerome (1889)

DORADE
All This and Sailing, Too
Olin Stephens (2000)
*Sparkman and Stephens: Giants
of Classic Yacht Design*
Franco Pace (2002)
The Great Classic Yacht Revival
Nic Compton (2004)

CASANOVA'S GONDOLA
The Story of My Life
Giacomo Casanova (1822)
The Gondola Maker
Laura Morelli (2014)

MEGAN JAYE
Nowhere Man
Robert Rosen (2006)

ARABIA
By Felucca Down the Nile
Willard Price (1940)

AVENGER
Sailing, Seamanship & Yacht Construction
Uffa Fox (1937)
Best of Uffa
ed. by Guy Cole (1978)

GYPSY MOTH IV
Gypsy Moth Circles the World
Sir Francis Chichester (1967)
Gipsy Moth IV: A Legend Sails Again
Paul Gelder (2007)

CORMORANT
The Voyage of the Cormorant
Christian Beamish (2013)
www.thecleanestline.com
/christian-beamish

EGRET
The Commodore's Story
Ralph Middleton Munroe (1930)
www.woodenboat.com
/boat-plans-kits/sharpie-315-egret

SERAFFYN
Seraffyn's Mediterranean Adventure
Lin & Larry Pardey (1971)
Cruising in Seraffyn
Lin & Larry Pardey (1976)
Seraffyn's Oriental Adventure
Lin & Larry Pardey (1985)
As Long as It's Fun
Herb McCormick (2013)

TILIKUM
*The Venturesome Voyages
of Captain Voss*
John C. Voss (1913)

JOSHUA
The Long Route
Bernard Moitessier (1971)
A Voyage for Madmen
Peter Nichols (2002)
Sailing Solo
Nic Compton (2003)
Moitessier: A Sailing Legend
Jean-Michel Barrault (2005)

SAID
www.bills-log.blogspot.co.uk/2009
/11/tribute-to-evgeny-gvozdev.html

LIBERIA III
Alone at Sea
Dr Hannes Lindemann (1958)

KATHENA NUI
Voices from the Sea
Nic Compton (2007)
www.wilfried-erdmann.de

CRUSOE'S PERIAGUA
*The Life and Most Surprising Adventures
of Robinson Crusoe, of York, Mariner*
Daniel Defoe (1719)

CHIDIOCK TICHBORNE
*A Single Wave: Stories of Storms
and Survival*
Webb Chiles (1995)
Storm Passage: Alone Around Cape Horn

Webb Chiles (1977)
The Ocean Waits
Webb Chiles (1984)
The Open Boat: Across the Pacific
Webb Chiles (1982)
www.inthepresentsea.com

DOVE/RETURN OF DOVE
Dove
Robin Lee Graham &
Derek T. Gill (1973)
Home Is the Sailor
Robin Lee Graham (1983)

TINKERBELLE
Tinkerbelle
Robert Manry (1967)
www.robertmanryproject.com

HŌKŪLEʻA
*Hawaiki Rising: Hokuleʻa, Nainoa
Thompson, and the Hawaiian
Renaissance*
Sam Low (2013)
www.hokulea.com
www.pvs.kcc.hawaii.edu

IDUNA
Taking on the World
Ellen MacArthur (2003)
www.ellenmacarthur.com

FIRECREST
Firecrest Round the World
Alain Gerbault (1981)

SQUEAK
Three Years in a 12-foot Boat
Stephen G. Ladd (2000)

AMERICA
The Low Black Schooner
John Rousmaniere (1987)
*The Official Book: America's Cup Jubilee
2001*, ed. by Nic Compton (2001)

GUPPY
One Girl, One Dream
Laura Dekker (2015)

BLUENOSE
Schooner Bluenose
Andrew Merkel (1948)
Bluenose II
L.B. Jenson (1994)
A Race for Real Sailors
Keith McLare (2006)

CHRISTIANIA
From Sail to Water-jet
Bjørn Foss (2005)

KON-TIKI
The Kon-Tiki Expedition
Thor Heyerdahl (1950)

FRAM
Farthest North
Fridtjof Nansen (1897)

GJØA
The North-West Passage
Roald Amundsen (1898)
The Search for the North-west Passage
Ann Savours (2003)

Index

Acknowledgements

Thanks to Kate Shanahan at The Ivy Press for persevering with a good idea,
and Jamie Pumfrey and Tom Kitch for guiding it through the production hoops so effortlessly.
Also to Lin and Larry Pardey for supplying the map of their journey—not to mention providing
inspiration for my own boatbuilding efforts.

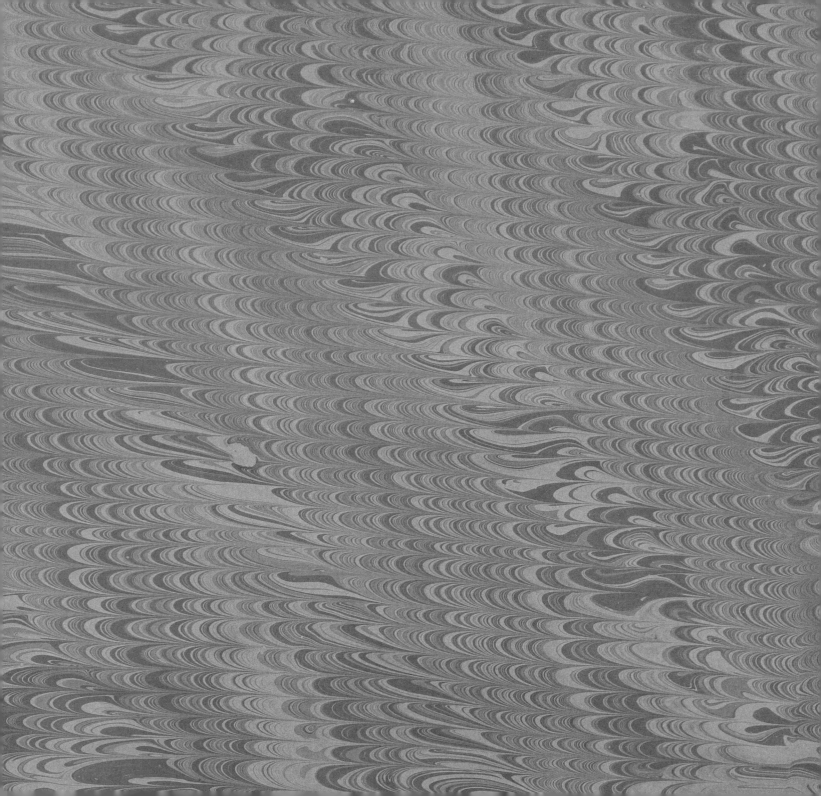